BASICS
FASHION MANAGEMENT

Virginia Grose

A Practical Guide to the Fashion Industry

Concept to Customer

Second Edition

BLOOMSBURY VISUAL ARTS

LONDON · NEW YORK · OXFORD · NEW DELHI · SYDNEY

BLOOMSBURY VISUAL ARTS
Bloomsbury Publishing Plc
50 Bedford Square, London, WC1B 3DP, UK
1385 Broadway, New York, NY 10018, USA

BLOOMSBURY, BLOOMSBURY VISUAL ARTS and the Diana
logo are trademarks of Bloomsbury Publishing Plc

First edition published in 2012
This second edition published in 2021

A catalogue record for this book is available from the British Library.

Library of Congress Cataloging-in-Publication Data
Names: Grose, Virginia, author.
Title: A practical guide to the fashion industry : concept to customer / Virginia Grose.
Other titles: Concept to customer
Description: Second edition. | New York : Bloomsbury Publishing (UK), 2021. | Series:
Basics fashion management | Includes bibliographical references and index.
Identifiers: LCCN 2020033517 (print) | LCCN 2020033518 (ebook) | ISBN
9781350079670 (paperback) | ISBN 9781350079687 (pdf)
Subjects: LCSH: Fashion merchandising.
Classification: LCC HD9940.A2 G76 2021 (print) | LCC
HD9940.A2 (ebook) | DDC 746.9/2--dc23
LC record available at https://lccn.loc.gov/2020033517
LC ebook record available at https://lccn.loc.gov/2020033518

ISBN: PB: 978-1-3500-7967-0
ePDF: 978-1-3500-7968-7
ePub: 978-1-3502-2739-2

Series: Basics Fashion Management

Printed and bound in India

To find out more about our authors and books visit
www.bloomsbury.com and sign up for our newsletters.

Introduction v

1

Context and Concept 1
From couture to high street 2
Designer typology 7
Research and idea generation 11
Trend forecasting 21
Interview: Emily Gordon-Smith 25
Case study: EDITED 28
Chapter summary 32

2

Product Development 35
The role of design in business 36
The product mix 40
Garment specifications: sampling 46
Interview: Steven Tai 50
Case study: MATCHESFASHION.COM 53
Chapter summary 63

3

Retail Strategy 65
Defining retail strategy 66
Implementing retail strategy 69
The marketing mix: position 71
The marketing mix: place 72
The marketing mix: price 74
The marketing mix: people 76
Interview: Richard Hurtley 84
Case study: Farfetch 87
Chapter summary 90

4

The Fashion Supply Chain 93
Background of the textile industry and
    supply chains 94
What is fast fashion? 95
Global sourcing and world class supply
    chain models 100
Sustainability in fashion supply chains 107
Risk measures and controls in fashion
    supply chains 111
Logistics and outsourcing in the supply
    chain 113
Interview: Liz Leffman 114
Case study: Kering Group 117
Chapter summary 120

5

Fashion Brands 123
Customer profiling 124
Building a brand 127
Luxury brands 127
Mass market and fast fashion brands 129
Storytelling and brand promotion 134
Brand protection 136
Interview: Paul Alger 139
Case study: The British House 144
Chapter summary 149

Conclusion 150
Glossary 152
Bibliography 154
Useful Websites 156
Index 157
Picture credits 162
Acknowledgements 164

Room

HEALTHIO
IN(3D)USTRY

16-18 OCTOBER 2019

Since the first edition of this book was written, the landscape of the fashion industry has changed significantly; in some ways, beyond recognition.

According to Joanne Yulan Jong in her 2018 text *The Fashion Switch*, there has been a 'click' moment in the fashion business, *click* being the sound of the fashion business changing from *transmit* to *receive*, where the focus has shifted to what the customer wants instead of having it dictated to them. This change is influenced by the digital revolution and the need for sustainability – two very different factors.

The second edition of this text highlights the key changes whilst emphasizing that the steps required of the basics of fashion management are still, in essence, the same ones Charles Frederick Worth took when creating 'fashion', and when I studied fashion design in the 1980s. The way we now carry out the creative process and the speed at which we work and, most importantly, the tools used may have changed.

The fashion industry encompasses anything sold in a fashion retail store, virtually, online or physically with a recognizable brand name. Fashion designers are product managers and innovators; they might work on a freelance or independent basis or as part of a larger design team, such as in a retail business or within the supply chain at a manufacturer's headquarters. The business of fashion is not built on the design function alone: areas such as forecasting, product development, manufacturing, retailing, marketing, branding and promotion combine to create a multi-billion dollar industry that employs millions worldwide.

However, some of the roles are now merged or blurred; for example, lines between design and buying or buying and merchandising, and the skills required, may be different. Like never before, most retailers want staff that can create or contribute to online content and to the marketing and story of the brand.

0.1 **3D Printed Clothing Exhibition**
A visitor is seen admiring clothes and fabrics made with 3D technology.

Much like the products and designs that are created, each function within this vast industry is unique. New opportunities in new markets continue to open up in the fashion industry, because customers still want to grab a bargain, purchase something unique, or be seen wearing the latest trends. Fashion design and product development adds value to a retailer or fashion brand's business. However, the industry needs innovation, generated at the same rate as product consumption, or it will become stale; the fashion industry is one that plans for its products to become obsolete at the end of each season.

The industry has evolved due to the digital revolution, extending its reach from product design to selling and promotion, and influence from movers and shakers – the bloggers and key opinion leaders (KOLs) are prevalent. However, the product needs to be 'right' and customers are more demanding; meanwhile, the promotion of product requires great images, great campaigns and overall a great story.

Beyond the excitement and gloss, the fashion industry is one of the most polluting in the world. Sustainability has emerged as an essential aspect of the fashion business and is not 'nice to have'. Sustainability should be integrated into everything we do in the fashion business, from recycled packaging to ethical manufacturing. We must ensure we are paying a fair wage to workers throughout the supply chain whilst constantly seeking out innovative new materials that can help preserve our planet and its precious resources. As Andrew Morgan asks in his film *The True Cost*, 'Where will we throw fashion clothing away – when there is no 'away'?'

'We behave as a start-up which means that innovation drives everything we do, from implementing cutting-edge design techniques to inventing more sustainable ways to make our products, to open-sourcing our sustainability innovations to the rest of the industry.'
– Michael Kobori, Levi's CEO

One of the biggest challenges the fashion business faces around sustainability is its culture. In order for our industry to become truly sustainable, we cannot just pick and choose practices that are easy and convenient to implement – every part of its operations needs to change. To tackle this challenge properly, a complete shift in business culture is needed. In fact, it should be the first step in creating a new mindset that puts sustainability at the heart of all decision making. Thinking sustainably means from the conception of the product and design through to delivery and post purchase. The 'circular economy' approach is discussed in more detail in Chapter 4: The Fashion Supply Chain. Levi's is a fashion brand that has attempted to embed sustainability through cultural change, according to the CEO Michael Kobori.

The fashion business continues to evolve as retailers create new roles within the industry: buyers and merchandisers, product developers, sourcing managers, textile and fabric technologists are some of the industry's key roles. All of this means that for today's graduates there are many opportunities for varied career paths in the fashion business all over the world and within different types of organization. New roles have evolved in the last few years, which creates more opportunities in this varied industry. These include digital analysts and digital scientists in fashion, as well as influencer marketers, sustainability managers, ecommerce controllers, styling editors, online personal stylists and resale fashion experts.

The speed of this evolution has highlighted a number of emerging, important considerations for the industry, including issues surrounding sustainability and ethics. The appetite for fast fashion set by certain brands is yet to slow down, as too is consumer enthusiasm for designer goods and branded products within the luxury goods sector. However, the importance of reuse and recycling has emerged and a more sustainable fashion industry shows signs of developing. The fashion business is polarized as the need for new exciting product and planned change is ever present, yet it is more important than ever that we utilize resources wisely and plan for reuse and sustainability into each stage.

The business of fashion should be viewed as a critical path; however, we need to view it as a circular and not a linear process, one that puts back in as well as takes out resources such as packaging and raw materials. Each milestone in the fashion system and critical path, from concept to customer, is specifically designed to add value to the product. However, the process is moving beyond the current take-make-dispose extractive industrial fashion business model to a circular one that aims to redefine growth, focusing on positive society-wide benefits. It entails gradually decoupling economic activity from the consumption of finite resources and designing waste out of the system. Underpinned by a transition to renewable energy sources, the circular model builds economic, natural, and social capital.

According to Ellen Macarthur, the concept of a Circular Economy is based on three principles:

× To design out waste and pollution
× Keep products and materials in use
× Regenerate natural systems

(Source, Ellen Macarthur Foundation, 2018)

These should be embedded into the fashion critical path and considered at each stage. The key stages in this fashion product development critical path are:

× Concept, trend and idea generation
× Design strategy
× Design and product development
× Retail strategy
× Fabric development – consider renewed and recycled materials
× Sampling and costing
× Range planning
× Sourcing strategy
× Production
× Shipping
× Distribution
× Promotion
× Sales
× Customer reaction
× Reuse
× Return
× Recycle

This is a generic pathway: every fashion retailer or brand should adapt and develop its own version to ensure that they are tailored to the requirements of its product ranges and customer base.

The aim of this book is to recreate this blueprint for fashion design, marketing, buying and merchandising so that you gain an appreciation of the critical path and key stages of the fashion business. Each of the five chapters explores a milestone in the fashion pathway. To help bring the theory to life and make the content immediately accessible, each chapter also contains a relevant case study and an interview with an industry professional. There are also self-reflective questions and exercises at the end of each chapter to help you to develop their ideas further.

0.2 **The Circular Fashion Critical Path**

FASHION CRITICAL PATH

Research and idea generation

Initial concept

Range planning

Range designs sign-off

Fabric and yarn development

Sample sign-off

Manufacturing

Shipment of bulk production

Distribution to stores

Visual merchandising

Sales and customer experience

Context
and Concept

This chapter will provide an insight into the creative activities and design concepts of the fashion process. The creative activities in any business setting will form part of a broader operational process that is designed to turn innovative and intangible ideas into a profitable reality. The fashion industry is no exception. Creating fashion is an exciting, challenging and often risky business, but this highly creative industry is underpinned by solid business models and operational workflow. It is important to bear in mind that any retailer is in the fashion business to make a profit, and that fashion is a for-profit industry like any other.

1.1 Concept Stages
A designer's workplace showing their sketches, swatches and ideation to creating a range.

From couture to high street

The process of the fashion business remains much the same now as when Charles Frederick Worth introduced the concept of haute couture in the 1850s: an idea is sketched to start the ball rolling and samples are made; then the garments are manufactured and sold to individual or mass-market customers. He was the first person to put labels with his name inside clothes to denote their authenticity, and indeed a brand name.

Haute couture and prêt-à-porter

Haute couture specifically refers to the design and construction of high-quality clothes by leading fashion houses. In its purest form, the term is a protected appellation. A certain number of formal criteria (such as number of employees or participation in fashion shows) must be met for a fashion house to use the label. Christian Dior, Chanel, Balmain, Balenciaga, Gucci and Givenchy were originally set up as haute couture design houses. In broader usage, the term couture is used to describe all custom-made clothing.

Couture designers and luxury brands and their design houses occupy a highly influential position in the fashion process; they are often the first to identify and capture a trend, concept or theme, which other designers and stakeholders in the fashion business then emulate for creative or commercial gain. Many of the pieces that couture designers create are arguably works of art. These creations are eventually translated into wearable, commercial and fashionable clothes suitable for mass-market consumption. To keep the fashion business cycle in motion, it is essential to invest in and nurture the talent and innovation of pure creative designers at this level.

Prêt-à-porter (ready-to-wear) clothing lines were the first radical alternative to couture pieces when they hit boutiques in the 1960s. The term describes factory-made clothing that is sold in finished condition and in standardized sizes (as distinct from bespoke, made-to-measure haute couture). Yves Saint Laurent (YSL) is credited as being the first French haute couturier to come out with a full prêt-à-porter line; some attribute this decision as a wish to democratize fashion, although other couture houses were preparing prêt-à-porter lines at the same time. The first Rive Gauche stores, which sold the YSL prêt-à-porter line, opened in Paris in 1966.

Charles Frederick Worth (1826–1895)

Widely credited with introducing the concept of haute couture, Charles Worth was known for preparing designs that were shown on live models and tailor-made for clients in his workshop. Worth was not the first or only designer to organize his business in this way, but his aggressive self-promotion earned him recognition as the first 'couturier'.

1.2 **New Look**

Christian Dior's New Look (1947) was controversial because the collection used vast amounts of fabric in a period when wartime rationing was still in effect. Christian Dior defined a new business model in the post-war years, establishing ready-to-wear boutiques and licensing deals; his designs were copied and sold in the USA as well as Europe. Many consider Dior's model to be a forerunner of fast fashion. In this image, Suzy Parker is wearing a rose chiffon gathered bodice and black tulip-pleat skirt, with pillbox and wrap jacket, by Dior.

> 'Often what seems to be intuition is actually clever assimilation and analysis of careful research.'
> – Gini Stephens Frings, 2002

Ready-to-wear has rather different connotations in the spheres of fashion and classic clothing. In the fashion industry, designers produce ready-to-wear clothes that are intended to be worn without significant alteration, because clothing made to standard sizes will fit most people. Standard patterns and faster construction techniques are used to keep costs down, compared to a custom-sewn version of the same item. Some fashion houses and designers offer mass-produced, industrially manufactured ready-to-wear lines, while others offer garments that, while not unique, are produced in limited numbers.

The influence of couture houses and designers has changed over time. Nowadays, only a very small clientele can afford the time and expense demanded by true couture clothing. Instead, the iconic fashion houses of Chanel, Givenchy, Dior, Gucci, Balenciaga, Balmain, Dolce & Gabbana, Ralph Lauren and Armani make a larger proportion of their profits from licensing agreements on cosmetics, perfume and accessories. For example,

Chanel's Rouge Noir lipstick and nail polish brought the House of Chanel to the masses and sales of its cosmetics and perfume are worth billions of dollars. Gucci decided to target millennial customers recently and repositioned their brand to directly target a younger, yet still affluent, ready-to-wear customer.

Fast fashion: the high-street revolution

Although we tend to think of fast fashion as a new industry initiative, it is, in fact, a redevelopment and refinement of Yves Saint Laurent's prêt-à-porter business model. Chain store retailers began to emerge in the 1960s, such as Mary Quant, Chelsea Girl and Biba in the UK and Levi Strauss and Gap in the USA.

Today's top designers, many of whom are now household names, influence the fashion industry as a whole. Designer or 'luxury' brands such as Giorgio Armani, Calvin Klein and Ralph Lauren are examples of large businesses that develop products for the mass market via their diffusion ranges and high-street collaborations. The distinction between high-end and mass-market fashion is blurring as collaborations between designers and high-street stores have become commonplace. This trend is driven by high consumer demand for fast fashion. If the masses cannot afford the original then the designers are prepared to go the masses. This and the concept of 'masstige' will be discussed further in Chapter 5.

1.3 Designer Creations and High-Street Copycats
Blogger Kaveh Moghaddam wearing a Gucci silver crackle bomber jacket in Dusseldorf Germany, a jacket that was then replicated for the highstreet by Forever 21.

The fashion industry is one of the few industries to provide advance images (via the Internet) of its new product ranges and, by doing so, it can be argued that designer houses are providing a form of service to the high-street fashion retailers via their creative influence. The media and fashion press are responsible for editing the collections and presenting trends along with the catwalk spreads and advance product information in their online publications and via social media. Such catwalk creations are then filtered down (at speed) to mass market fashion retail. Much of the fashion media, for example, will regularly feature 'copycat' sections, showing the public where to find cheaper, replica versions of designer items. The impact of influencers and bloggers in fashion and the breadth of information provided to the public at large has added to the impact of replication in the fashion industry on the industry.

Something that begins its life on a drawing board at a fashion house may easily become a derivative version in Zara, H&M or Topshop. The $3,400 Gucci silver bomber jacket is an example of this and was developed into a $34.90 Forever 21 style. This distinctive design was interpreted by high-street design teams, making it suitable for mass production at an affordable purchase price.

'To keep her attention, there has to be fresh goods with new deliveries. We live in an ADD (attention deficit disorder) society.'
– The Business of Fashion, Lauren Sherman, 2017

However, such 'copycat' designs are not confined to the mass market; luxury brands have also been accused of copying small new designers' ideas in their collections. Chanel has admitted that some of the Fair Isle sweaters in its runway collection were closely inspired by pieces that Chanel staff had bought from Mati Ventrillon, a designer from the Shetland Islands in Scotland.

1.4 See Now Buy Now
The Burberry Ready to Wear Spring/Summer 2020 fashion show during London Fashion Week September 2019, London.

The 'See Now Buy Now' business model

See Now Buy Now (SNBN) is a business model that is not completely new to the fashion world. There are many companies that historically were able to make the product available very soon after its presentation on the catwalks or in the showrooms. We can consider many examples coming from fast-fashion, including companies that are pure online players who are used to satisfying customers' requests right after the publication of a new item on the web. This model has now been adopted by the luxury market as SNBN. The Burberry business model was the first of the luxury brands to do this, legitimizing it as well as the irrationality of separating the presentation of men's and women's collections. See Now Buy Now actually means reinterpreting both the essence of collection and the approach to physical distribution, this latter in coherence with an omnichannel view of the fashion world.

In the original fashion system the cycle of selling was an anachronism – clothes were shown in February and not made available for six months. At that point, images were available online and consumers needed to wait. This has changed over the last few years in line with the speed of digital media. Driven by Burberry, many others have followed such as Rebecca Minkoff and Vetements.

Enablers of See Now Buy Now

There are essentially three fundamentals for making See Now Buy Now possible, according to Alessandro Brun et al.:

1. **Time compression along the whole set of processes**: The critical path for development and production has to be shorter. What is presented and immediately sold is not a self-standing collection; it rather offers an initial taste of the main collection that will be in stores some months later, hence they have the same design origin.

2. **Localized manufacturing proximity of sourcing**: Reshoring is a fundamental issue in fashion, especially for brands who are sensitive to the 'made in' critical success factor. However, among the major reasons it is convenient to manufacture close to the destination markets is the necessity of speeding up deliveries. If the product is already close to the market – either in the warehouse or as a work-in-process – this becomes a condition for making possible the immediate delivery right after the presentation on catwalks or showrooms.

3. **Optimization of sourcing and production**: The adaptation of lean techniques to the production floors can improve the time performance of about 30 percent and take lead time down to two weeks.

This means that if the sales campaign lasts three weeks, it is possible to launch production right at the beginning of the campaign.

(Source: Brun, Alessandro & Castelli, Cecilia & Karaosman, Hakan, 2017)

> 'The fashion system has been reconfigured and this aims to remove the traditional calendar of fashion to make collections immediately available for purchase.'
> – Wischover, 2016

Designer typology

Fashion designers develop new concepts and, as part of the creative process, are responsible for delivering these concepts in the form of fashionable clothing designs. There are different types of fashion designers and fashion retailers worldwide and they work in different segments of the market, such as fashion branding, design houses or high-street retail. Designers from different sectors of the fashion business influence one another; they are inextricably linked by the design process and take inspiration from everywhere and everything that they come into contact with.

Rieple and Gander (2009) conducted research on the typology of fashion designers and arrived at the conclusion that there are four classifications into which most apparel designers fall: mavericks, leaders, interpreters and reproducers.

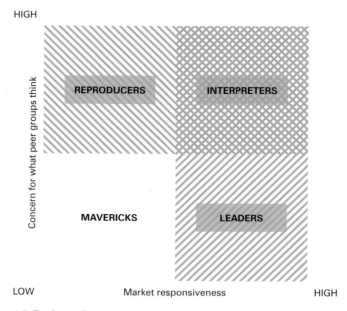

1.5 Designer Typology
This is a typology of designers in the fashion business as devised by Rieple & Gander, 2009.

Designers are inextricably linked by the design process and each other. Research by Rieple and Gander focuses on designer typology and how co-locating with other designers and creative organizations allows them to draw upon a number of intangible resources such as street scenes, social moods and atmosphere in order to create new designs (Rieple & Gander, 2009).

These typologies are still evolving in the industry and impact on the roles of buying and merchandising and marketing as brands and retailers take a more rounded view of business to match the 24/7 switched on digital environment.

Mavericks

Mavericks are purely creative (rather than commercial) designers and often assume the role of creative design director or trend-forecasting consultant. Mavericks advise top design houses on directions for colour, style and fabric choices. These designers are not primarily concerned with current consumer or market trends; they will instead create couture, new looks and direction for a brand, preferring to lead rather than follow. Examples of contemporary mavericks include John Galliano, Vivienne Westwood, and Alessandro Michele at Gucci. Brands can consider the type of media attention these names attract.

1.6 Moodboards

In this image we see a designer creating her initial moodboard, an important part of the creation and concept process.

Leaders

Fashion leaders are 'top-end' designers who become recognizable names during the course of their career by either working for other fashion houses (such as Raf Simons at Dior and then subsequently until recently Calvin Klein, Olivier Rousteing at Balmain) or by setting up a commercial, rather than purely creative, business model. Leaders innovate in a highly fashionable and groundbreaking manner and will often establish their own label; for example, designer Tom Ford went on to develop his own label following his time at Gucci and went from being a marketeer to a designer name in his own right. Alessandro Michele has transformed Gucci into a brand for Millennials.

Interpreters

Interpreters have assumed a relatively new role in fashion. They are neither designers nor buyers or product developers, but a hybrid of all three. These individuals have a commercial eye and are primarily concerned with selecting the key looks for a range or collection. Interpreters work closely with the merchandising and technical aspects of the business and will focus their energies on the way in which a brand or retailer communicates their design message to consumers. Examples of companies that employ interpreters include: Reiss, Karen Millen, All Saints, Anthropologie and Ted Baker. Additionally, large multiples or retailer brands, including those online with in-house labels, such as Net a Porter, Matches and ASOS and Boden also employ fashion interpreters.

Reproducers

Reproducers (also known as fast fashion designers) work in conjunction with a team of buyers and product developers, managing the development of the looks for a particular retailer or brand. They ensure that colour palettes and trends of the looks fit with the business or brand. These commercially astute designers need to ensure that whilst the direction is 'fashion right' it is simultaneously wearable and cost-effective. Reproducers source, select and adapt ideas and trends to suit a particular segment of the market. It is arguably not a highly creative role, yet it is a technically skilful one required to highlight those catwalk trends that will successfully translate to the high street. Mass market retailers such as H&M, Zara, Topshop and Forever 21 employ such reproducers. The use of Trend Forecasting services is a crucial resource for reproducers who work at such speed in this segment.

'The best way to predict the future is to create it.'
– Peter Drucker

Research and idea generation

The creative process of fashion design does not have a fixed start or end point; it is an iterative process and fashion designers often display magpie tendencies by constantly seeking and collecting sources of inspiration in order to rework, evolve and advance their ideas in a cyclical way. Sources of inspiration may include a scrap of fabric, a flash of colour, a trip to another city or country, or an exhibition; equally, there may be an accumulation of different ideas gathered over time.

Designers find inspiration almost anywhere and the interpretation of that inspiration is often where the magic and innovation begins, for example, if we take a look at those red-soled Louboutin shoes. Christian Louboutin's red soles were initially inspired by Andy Warhol and a bottle of nail varnish. When designing a pair of shoes influenced by Warhol's Flowers, Louboutin was dissatisfied with the outcome. While looking at the shoes, which had black soles, to try to figure out why they didn't work, his assistant was painting her nails red. Seeing the polish, Louboutin lacquered the shoe's sole, and an icon was born. Inspiration and where it comes from is the very essence of the

1.7 Christian Louboutin
Christian Louboutin shoe brand showing their iconic red soles which have become the symbol of luxury shoes; however, the original concept design was conceived from painting soles with red nail polish by Louboutin.

fashion design process and continual research is a critically important success factor in developing and determining new design concepts.

Commercial fashion designers have to conceive and develop fashion ranges and remain creative whilst working closely with buyers, merchandisers and senior managers in order to successfully channel a company's message and philosophy into its clothing. The process involves analyzing key trends from the catwalk shows and identifying opportunities to translate these ideas into clothing that will fit a company's brand.

Forecasting trends and developing inspired ideas based upon information gathered is not new. It is vital to fashion designers to find continual new sources of inspiration. Originality and flair are key prerequisites for a fashion designer's creativity. These intangible qualities cannot be easily taught and are instead forged by a designer's intuition and translated into their clothing style, which makes research and trend forecasting such an exciting area of the creative process.

Market analysis and research

The behaviour of customers dictates to retailers how to develop successful new products and gives a great insight (if correctly analyzed) into customer shopping habits and behaviour. Historical data has often been a dictator of future trends so it should be no surprise that the creative process in fashion retailing often begins with analyzing consumer trend data, sales information and customer feedback from the previous season. Retailers also routinely consult market research services (such as Stylus, WGSN,

EDITED, Marketline) in order to define the competition and further analyze the market and environmental trend factors that are most relevant to their customers. Market research provides an invaluable insight into the industry; data is combined with other key macro-environmental influences (the key drivers affecting both the retailer or business and its customers) to help designers capture the spirit of the times, the fashion zeitgeist, when developing their collections (Stone, 2001). Equally, there can be a paradigm shift such as the burgeoning need for sustainability in the fashion cycle and move to a circular economy.

Zeitgeist Examples

The fashion zeitgeist can further be defined by:

× A designer's signature or style influence (such as Alessandro Michele at Gucci)
× A style icon or celebrity (such as Rihanna, Kanye West or Victoria Beckham)
× A fashion look, maybe created by film or TV (think of Carrie from Sex and the City and the wardrobe created by Pat Field)
× A bohemian element found in music or street culture (emulating rappers such as Jay-Z)
× A fashion model (for example, Gigi Hadid or Kaia Gerber)
× Advances in fibre or fabric technology (for example, Lycra developments in the 1970s made body-conscious clothing fashionable and Adidas recently made sneakers from plastic fishing nets)

(Adapted Source: E L Brannon, 2005)

1.8 Designer Pat Field and Kim Cattrall
Attending the film premiere of Sex and the City 2 at Radio City, New York.

1.9 Adidas X Kanye West Yeezy
Rhianna attends the celebrity and designer collaboration launch party of Adidas and Kanye West's brand Yeezy.

1.10 Amazon Fashion Week
A guest seen during the Amazon Fashion Week in Tokyo, 2019.

Colour information

In addition to customer and market research, designers visit yarn and fabric trade fairs and attend seminars year round in order to compile initial colour palettes and fabric and trim ideas for their range planning.

It is vital to have this research information to hand when fashion designers are putting pen to paper so that as silhouettes are developed, they are linked to and supported by the appropriate fabric and trim information. The initial design, concept and product development processes do not work independently of one another.

Directional and comparative shopping

Shopping takes on a whole new meaning for commercial designers. Designers travel to the aforementioned trade fairs and designer, high street and vintage stores and street markets in order to seek out ideas from around the globe. Equally, this research can happen online and is quicker; the many trend sites and bloggers and influencers sites are good sources. This is known as directional shopping and research. Notes and images will be taken and sometimes samples are bought for further analysis of fabric trim or styling direction. Often garments will be deconstructed (literally ripped apart) to analyze and test fabrics so that they may be redeveloped and recreated into mass market products. Fabric mills and yarn spinners may be visited to discuss and develop specific fabrics and fibres suitable for the brand. These may include innovative recycled and reused elements such as 'old' fabric from garment recycling or even ocean plastics and bottles.

Comparative shopping and competitive analysis helps buyers and commercial designers to determine the retailer's position in the marketplace; the process highlights similarities or differences between a retailer and its competition. Factors such as price, styling and quality will be observed and reviewed, as will any promotional activity. Comparative shopping provides a snapshot of the competition – and it is an important part of the commercial design process. In-store visits to see physical layouts and brand adjacencies remain crucial as part of this process.

Trade Fairs

The following key fashion, fabric, yarn and product fairs help determine the look of any given product range. Many of these remain bi-annual, falling in January/February and September/October.

However, pre-collection fashion weeks and the move to See Now Buy Now in the industry has created a shift to all year round product 'drops' from all brands. This extends to the luxury brands and in some ways, the luxury market mirrors fast fashion brands in this manner.

× London Fashion Week
× Paris Fashion Week
× New York Fashion Week
× Milan Fashion Week
× Tokyo Fashion Week
× Première Vision (Paris, France)
× Pitti Filati (Florence, Italy)
× Magic (Las Vegas, USA)
× Coterie New York

1.11 Premiere Vision Global Textile Show, Paris
Trade fairs are an essential part of the research process. Designers attend yarn and fabric trade fairs in order to compile colour and fabric palettes.

1.12 A Fashion Buyer Selecting Fabric
Buyers make selections as part of the commercial direction of the product development process, including choosing the fabrics.

Trends in the marketplace

In any commercial environment, trends in the marketplace will help shape the future direction of the business and help the organization to fulfil the needs and desires of the customer. The fashion business is no exception. Trends in business can be broadly categorized in one of three ways: macro, micro and megatrends.

Macro or environmental trends are driven by long-term societal, global and political forces, often referred to as the PESTEL model, representing political, economic, sociological, technological, environmental and legal forces. The retailer or company will decide which of these factors are the likely drivers or forces that will influence the whole of society and therefore individual customer behaviour. These trends can evolve over a long period of time, gather momentum and may be hugely influential for retailers. See more on the PESTEL model in Chapter 3, page 68.

Micro trends are more immediate; they can create a lot of interest or noise but tend to disappear as quickly as they arrive. The fashion industry is particularly affected and shaped by micro trends. These can be weather related, such as snow or a heatwave, or may be blips or fads that take off and die quickly, or remain and become classic items. A good example of a fashion-related trend that evolved in this way and has been in and out of fashion for decades is the 'all in one' or 'jumpsuit', which has its roots in the 1970s but has now become a classic fashion wardrobe item.

Macro and micro trends can evolve into what are widely known as megatrends. A megatrend will last longer, affect greater aspects of society than either macro or micro trends and may involve a complex process that can include global economic forces, political persuasions and technological advances. Megatrends have a lasting influence on society and can be unpredictable (Vejlgaard, 2007). Indeed, according to Vejlgaard, there are certain sectors of society that have historically driven (and continue to drive) megatrend development, such as the young, sub-cultures, artists, the wealthy or super-rich, designers, celebrities and the media. A good example of a megatrend is ethical fashion and sustainability in fashion, which has been evolving for over ten years and is now widely accepted as a 'way of life' and becoming 'business as usual' rather than merely a trend. Another includes 'wellness' the trend for yoga and exercise, a circle of healthy living and has clear links to athleisure wear.

Influencers and bloggers

The impact of social media and digitalization of the fashion industry has created another layer of influence and impact for designers to consider as part of the range planning and design process. These individuals with their large followers create trends and can make designers' names by wearing fashion, posting images on social media and writing about fashion creating content across a variety of media blogs and sites.

1.13 Street Style
Spotted in Milan, the influencer and fashion blogger Susanna Lau, also known as 'Susie Bubble', who has around half a million followers on Instagram.

Customer behaviour and segmentation

Commercial fashion design and retailing starts and ends with the customer. The customer is at the centre of all design developments and, simply put, the fashion business is the creation, interpretation and development of ideas to suit customers' needs. It is vital to keep this in mind: customer behaviour and consumer spending patterns drive the fashion industry.

Customer needs can be unpredictable, but it is important for designers to analyze sales and spending patterns as well as understand the key drivers of customer behaviour as part of the range or collection development process.

Digitalization of our world remains the biggest influence in the last decade on customer behaviour and designers and retailers alike have had to adapt in order to integrate major technological advances in their ranges and importantly, into their business models. Developing bespoke and customized products in fashion design and producing clothing that is suitable for customers, at the right price, is a continual challenge for fashion brands and retailers.

It is important to remember that the fashion industry is a commercial, for-profit business like any other and it begins and ends with the customer. Research into consumer behaviour and spending patterns drives the creation and development of innovative fashion to suit customer needs.

1.14 Fashion at Work
Designers are seen discussing ideas and presenting these to a potential buyer.

1.15 Textile Fair
Designers here are seen researching trends in fabric and colour.

Trend forecasting

The initial stages of the idea generation and range planning process are shaped by the fashion industry in the form of trend forecasting companies, major trade fairs and international trade panels that predict colour, fabric and styling for the season ahead. Trend forecasting is a vital part of the fashion design process; it provides the fuel in the fashion engine. However, the bloggers and key opinion leaders (KOLs) are setting trends and promoting ideas and product, which has become another major source of information about customers and inspiration if we consider social media as a whole and think of Instagram and Pinterest specifically.

The professional trend forecasters provide an invaluable service to large fashion retailers and brands, many of whom simply do not have sufficient time or resources to undertake this work in-house. Forecasters employ creative marketing and design consultants to predict trends and gather information for the fashion industry. These consultants will travel the globe seeking out concepts and trends that are taken from a wide range of sources such as music, street style, art, exhibitions, architecture and interior design.

Trend forecasting remains an important function within the fashion industry but it has evolved and changed with fashion itself. Some of the prestigious trend forecasting companies include (but are not limited to) WGSN, Promostyl,

'Fashion cannot exist without artistry; you can be commercial but need to inspire otherwise we lose what fashion is all about. For example, there has been some really good learning from social media and feminism slogans on Instagram. This has links with the evolution of fashion retail – the high street mass market is unrecognizable. Designers need to inspire people and use that magic and inspiration and also need to be good at learning by keeping a political ear to the ground.'
– Fran Sheldon, EDITED

EDITED, Stylus, Donegar, Trend Union and Peclers. These and other trend agencies will forecast everything from colour and styling to fabric and yarn. It is important to note that trend agencies do not forecast the construction of sample garments, which is exclusive to individual businesses and retailers. Retailers of designed products control this segment of the development process by working directly with manufacturers and suppliers. Newer sources include EDITED, are data driven and provide analytics and in some cases use artificial intelligence (AI) to provide real-time information to support fashion businesses' product developments.

Trends in colour direction act as a catalyst for further research into fabric and styling. Trend, colour and fashion forecasters often work two years in advance of the season. This seems at odds with the immediacy of the world we live in but colour evolves and is arguably an easier element to forecast than specific fabric and fashion design. Many trend forecasters have fashion design or research backgrounds, but increasingly data analytics and business acumen are equally important, as is the inherent curiosity to seek out the new, the original and the different.

Cool hunting

Most large organizations and retailers go to great lengths to stay ahead of the competition. One way in which they can do this is to employ 'cool hunters' to seek out trends and innovative ideas; this helps to ensure that they are the first to market with a great new product and can also help the organization develop a long-term strategy for its business.

Driven by a stiff level of market competition and most organizations' desire to get their product quickly to market and 'right' on the first attempt, the role of the cool hunter is rapidly assuming a key position in the fashion business. There are now many web-based forecasting and cool hunting companies or agencies. Brands such as Levi Strauss, Coca Cola and Nike are well known for using cool hunters to work on innovative projects, and many retailers use their own cool hunters to try to win the innovation race.

Cool hunters will observe and talk to trendsetters from all walks of life in order to find out what sociologists have referred to as the 'tipping point' (Gladwell, 2008) in the process of change.

1.16 Fashion in the Age of Technology
Karolina Kurkova wears a dress designed with
artificial intelligence at 'Manus x Machina:
Fashion in an Age of Technology' held at the
Costume Institute Gala at the Metropolitan
Museum of Art, 2016.

Finding trend-spotting clues is very
important to fashion designers and
retailers. The industry relies upon new
product development (or reinvention)
and customers in fashion thrive upon
'newness'. The entire industry is driven by
the need to stand out from the crowd or
look different and original. Websites that
promote cool and new trends (from the
sublime to the ridiculous) are great places
to start looking for inspiration. Search
online for 'cool hunter' and 'trend hunter'
to find their websites.

'A trend forecaster needs
to sense the moment when
ideas from the fringes of
culture are taken on by
the mainstream consumer
then give an indication of
where they think that will
lead. Forecasters must
watch constantly for the
zeitgeist is changing and
how this might affect their
consumer and therefore
kind of product they want.'
– Holland, G and Jones, R, 2017

1.17 Mode City Fashion Trade Show, Paris
This trade show is for International Swimwear and Lingerie Brands to present to buyers.

1.18 Istanbul Fashion Week
Kim Mannino of WGSN seen speaking at a trend forecasting conference held in Turkey and sponsored by Mercedes Benz.

'Trend forecasting is a widely used but little understood skill in the fashion industry. It is important to remember that a forecast is not the same as a prediction and it is difficult to be precise when gazing into the future but should help shape future direction of design product development and brand image.'
– Holland, G and Jones, R, 2017

Interview

Emily Gordon-Smith has twenty-five years experience in fashion, spanning her editing and trend-forecasting background with brands and retailers on the creative direction side. She has worked with a vast mix of brands, including Zara, M&S, Target and Levis, managing a breadth of consultancy projects and also line managing buyers and designers.

Stylus encompasses: Forecasting Fashion, Beauty, and other Product Development and Styling – Emily heads up the fashion content but oversees the other directories as increasingly more trends take a cross-industry approach (for example sustainability and wellbeing) in the wider macro industry.

In your opinion, how has the role of the couture designer changed in the last 20 years to occupy its current position in the fashion industry?

It is less relevant and certainly very changed; if you think about new luxury and design houses designing streetwear, couture is more elevated and couture is much less relevant with the exception of a number of houses with new luxury exploring streetwear. We dress in such a generic way – menswear is similar, the traditional menswear design houses have struggled to create something relevant for customers. The world is so much more casual now in its approach to clothes and much more comfort focused. We are seeing a death of tailoring but some brands do show during couture week – for example Vetements is a brand that has helped create this shift and I think the whole role of luxury is changed.

Do you think the so-called 'top design houses' still influence fashion?

The role of couture and top designers are very rarefied roles and have much less influence in the industry unless it is through ready-to-wear, but look at how successful Gucci is. They are a great example of current success; they really have captured something of the moment with their spirit of young luxe consumer. Also, they have introduced a weekly committee of millennial consultants, which is super clever of Gucci to use this data to be informed and consulted by this new luxe consumer.

Most top design houses are suffering but certain brands have got it right. Brands such as these are not following a broad trend but are creating something completely unique – no one else is doing the same thing, it is not following a trend – we are seeing much more of a return to creativity. Something of the beautiful and crafted stands out and delivers something incredibly new.

Streetwear is key and this is where these top design houses influence when they tap into this trend, and it's a fact that everyone wants to dress more casually.

How do you think that current designers gather ideas and influences?

A great example of this is that now Gucci are consulting Millennials and conducting research in a new way – but brands overall are collecting information from street, nostalgia and celebrity culture. However, the impact coming from the street and less traditional content is more to do with more elevated culture, and cyclical trends very much exist. But instead of a 10-year cycle of trends there is this ad-hoc omni nostalgia that we can dip in and out of.

Do you think that yarn and fabric suppliers continue to be a large influence in the concept stages?

The BIG story here has to be sustainability – although there is much less influence in the broader stages but there are plenty of exciting things happening and this will rapidly be the case. Fashion brands and mills and manufacturers will be forced to behave more sustainably – this movement is really gaining momentum. Technical innovation – our hands are tied – a key pillar of content sustainability.

How does the media influence fashion in your opinion?

It really depends on age groups and younger audiences are crucial. The traditional media is suffering as it is all about social media where it's make or break with overnight trends linked to celebrity influences. The traditional fashion media is very sad – a much more analog way of gathering data – but does fit in with a nostalgia trend. Interesting but equally relevant that around 72 percent of Generation X are on Facebook – social media is not only for young people.

Given that colour forecasts tend to be conducted well in advance of a given season, do they remain relevant in the business of trend directions?

We do work 2.5 years ahead on colour and work globally with mills and manufacturers who also work so far ahead and there is no getting around it. However, we do also rely on colour forecasting much closer to the season with the retailers who provide a confirmation of what they are thinking and selling.

Do large, international high-street retailers take their inspiration from catwalks and trade fairs or from prediction companies or others?

They have huge volumes of information at their fingertips from all those resources and what is most important is to have a filter. Retailers need to take a bespoke approach and therefore much more edited and curated information is required. The industry moves so fast that they don't have enough time, and catwalk reporting is edited and is super hot. At Stylus we need to get into this detail for retailers and brands with our early confirmation resource. Trade fairs create more confirmation too and have an edited take on the situation. The retailers we work with want everything filtered for them to absorb information quickly; our role as forecasters has changed.

How do you think trend forecasting has changed and what is your view of trend forecasting for the future?

A physical shift from books to online services to technology stepping in has been a big trend in trend forecasting.

It is also not just about the product but everything around the product and lifestyle and how to stand out. *It has been a seismic shift.* There are also big opportunities to serve the modest (Muslim) customer and this presents a big opportunity for global brands.

TF is less about micro trends but includes the bigger questions impacting on customers. We now have a *season neutral strategy* and being flexible in how you supply products and sourcing more locally and closer to the season is crucial to provide shorter lead times. Destination wear sells well throughout the year and we do need a fast response in order to address the fashion calendar.

In terms of serving specific age groups such as 'middle age' is very easy to get this wrong. For example, a priority are details such as big pockets, comfort, and fabric quality as one gets older; it is an underserved market. In the future, TF will be much more about a macro level approach with the entire consumer lifestyle and understanding how this affects the industry.

How do you see luxury fashion brands and so-called 'celebrity designers' influencing the fashion industry as a whole?

This is a very interesting area, for example we are now seeing Virgil Abloh at Louis Vuitton and celebrities such as Jayzee for Puma. There is a trend that everyone can be a designer and whilst it may grate with industry and maybe there is an argument that they are technically more stylists than designers. But, absolutely, celebrity influence is there and it is also the zeitgeist – it is far more valuable to have celebrity associated with a brand than good quality of design, which was a traditional approach. However, we should acknowledge that it is possibly not a great message to the industry. Music and fashion and open source collaborations such as Adidas with a campaign using visual artists and musicians still has the integrity of product in mind. Some of the lines are very blurred in our industry and previous divisions and barriers have become less visible.

Case Study

EDITED: A Different Form of Forecasting

(This case study was taken from the author's interview with Fran Sheldon formerly of 'EDITED' and the EDITED website.)

In 2009 a new type of trend forecasting service to the fashion industry – EDITED – was founded in London by a programmer, Geoff Watts, and fashion designer, Julia Fowler. The current retail environment is a very crowded market where most designers and retailers don't have time to comparative shop manually. Trend forecasting really changed as a result of digitalization of the industry, according to Fran Sheldon, 'When EDITED arrived on the scene people did not know where to place it, they carved out whole new area and space in the industry but lots of other people have joined in and TF has moved from journalism to technology companies. We can only really talk about what is happening now and create data-fuelled information and not try too hard to predict the future. The future has to be made, it cannot be predicted – in the 1960s there were no predictions of smartphones or computers to be everywhere.'

EDITED identified an upheaval in trend forecasting linked to the entire fashion industry. For example, previously trend forecasting was a linear process and runways impacted on the high street in a direct 'trickle down' manner, whilst there was a clear 'bubble up' effect of street style. This is no longer a clear process and EDITED realized the opportunity of connectivity in forecasting through the digital and data revolution impacting the industry, for instance, the way that a brand such as Gucci has changed since the arrival of Alessandro Michele, who has created innovative products and takes his inspiration from, and is heavily engaged with, millennials and Gen Z.

In parallel with the digital revolution and 24/7 'connectedness' there has been a shake-up in the industry, manifesting itself in a merging of street style and runways via a mix of slick design to edgy sportswear looks and collaborations on products such as sneakers. This has also impacted on the sportswear industry with high fashion brands like Balenciaga competing directly with fashion brands. Also, the merging of different sectors such as music and fashion has created a broader threat as these sectors have become new competition and created disruptive innovation. Fashion trends and influences are fast moving and very fluid; the landscape is dynamic and the people running some of these newer brands – for example, Kim Kardashian West's 'Miss Kim' fashion brand – highlight this 'new' competition and diversity of brand and influences in the industry.

> **'The future has to be made, it cannot be predicted.'**
> – Fran Sheldon

EDITED understood that everyone carries a smartphone and are 'connected' in a way that had never previously existed. Customers of fashion brands are taking information provided by EDITED and following brands whilst going about their daily business. The data-driven services EDITED provides identified shifts in the environment linked to fashion trends for clients to help buyers and designers stay ahead and capitalize on these instantly.

Gathering ideas and inspiration
According to Sheldon, designers normally apply a mixture of inspiration from the world around them, including politics, but also look inwards for ideas. A designer must balance their own own identity with outside influences without becoming just one of the crowd.

Yarn and fabric suppliers continue to be influential in the concept stages and that inspiration is still important. For example, according to many in the fashion business inspiration is usually a mixture of magic and logic so traditional trend forecasts are still important, but they cannot tell you how to trade or retail or be commercial. This is where EDITED can help to bridge that gap with data based service and information, blending data with design concepts to support the product development and inspiration process.

Design houses influence on the fashion industry
Fashion cannot exist without artistry and designers can be commercial, but need to inspire; otherwise we can lose what fashion is all about. Some designers can become stuck in commerciality and risk their brand and identity being washed away by their products being sold

everywhere and becoming oversaturated. This has links with the evolution of retail – the high street has become unrecognizable since the digital revolution and those brands that have kept up with this are clear winners. Commercial designers need to continue to inspire people and use that magic and inspiration whilst learning by keeping a political ear to the ground. Fashion retailers often have own brands who wants to cut through the noise. The problem with many traditional big chains and department stores is the connectivity isn't there for customers who want to go directly to them online and expect a great experience.

Colour forecasting
EDITED works differently to the competition by showing retailers and brands what is happening now, so they can react to it instantly. For example, last year millennial pink was on trend in visual merchandising, but the garments did not sell as well as this trend's popularity would have suggested. So, it is important to note conversion of 'likes' on social media do not always convert into sales. EDITED informs brands through data what the window is for the sustainability of any look. The reality is that you cannot buy two years ahead and fashion brands need to have the next 'drop' of product ready and stay relevant by buying very close to the selected 'look'.

The media influence on trend forecasting
EDITED sees the media influence as part of digital connectivity and a part of their brand updating, being connected online, and reaching out to their audience. This means that from an influence perspective it used to be the media reporting on 'this

is what we are wearing this season', but this has now evolved into a 'what you could wear' reporting style which has a wider reach. EDITED works with most large international high-street retailers and most of these use a suite of inspiration and EDITED provides the data-price-product point of view. These can be linked with the more emotive predictions and brands that can combine the two are those likely to succeed.

Celebrity designers influence

The celebrity influence on fashion has come from a broad mix of industries, such as music, sport, film and TV. Many successful celebrity designers have a big following on social media, and a direct reach to their fans and potential customers for their new fashion lines and collaborations. Two obvious example are the Kardashians and Kanye West's Yeezy line and Victoria Beckham's luxury designer brand – very different celebrities from different industries, TV and music, but both incredibly successful.

The world of trend forecasting is complicated and the high-speed fashion industry relies on companies such as EDITED to translate influences and ideas into facts that they can edit further and personalize for their customers.

The user is still key

EDITED provides 'solid metrics' in fashion, using artificial intelligence techniques, to predict short-term sales trends. The mixture of AI and fashion is still in its infancy, and it remains to be seen if AI will replace some of the more traditional methods of fashion forecasting.

Most brands using trend forecasting services apply a mixture of influences, including big trend prediction services for inspiration. This mixture of information can help fashion brands to develop exciting commercial products. However, access to trend information is vital as part of a designer's concept creation, development and refinement process and trend forecasting is an aid to capturing the fashion zeitgeist. It is true that many retailers and brands use similar sources of concept and trend forecasting information as part of their initial development process. This has lead to a certain amount of homogenization in high-street stores and malls around the world, but the key for designers here is interpretation; ensuring that the key messages of the brand remain at the forefront of the product development process. It is vital to retain the design philosophy and brand integrity of individual fashion retailers. Equally, the use of big data can create more bespoke information that may be relevant to a brand, and if trend information needs this detailed analytical approach interpreted and reproduced in line with brand strategy. This detailed approach should help create the right looks and direction for the business. It is important to note that trend forecasting services and agencies are only as good as the designers, buyers and design teams who use them.

1.19 Kim Kardashian with Kanye West
Seen out in New York – style influencer and celebrity Kim Kardashian with her husband, the rapper and designer Kanye West.

Chapter summary

This chapter has dealt with the idea- and concept-development stage of the fashion business. We have discussed the initial planning stages and the importance of data gathering and have learned that there are different types of designers and retailers trying to cater to different customers' tastes and budgets. We have seen that concept and trend forecasting are part of the ingredients required to develop a vision and formalize the design strategy in the fashion business. However, it is important to note that all of the trend forecasting companies and fabric mills and trade fairs add to the 'tools' available to designers to use as and when required. These tools have evolved and been added to over the years and the mixture and magic of inspiration and seizing the zeitgeist in fashion is paramount to success.

Questions and discussion points

We have discussed the ways in which the industry develops its ideas. With this in mind consider the following questions:

1. What are the current macro-level influences affecting the fashion business as a whole? Are any of these mega or micro trends?

2. Which design houses and designers are currently influential to the fashion industry as a whole? Explain why.

3. How do mass-market retailers develop original fashion clothing without being accused of copying?

4. What are the different ways in which information can be gathered to create trends and forecast the fashion of the future?

5. How do you think the media including influencers and celebrities affect high-street fashion?

6. Which media and press do you notice that cover the catwalk collections in detail?

7. Write a list of the different ways in which ideas and directions for fashion clothing may be developed.

Exercises

Designers working on the high street have to pay the same attention to detail and channel their creativity just as much as those working in the couture houses. It is equally challenging to design a range of dresses to retail at under $100 (£60) as it is to design a bespoke piece for a client who desires an original item. These exercises are designed to help you channel your own creative thinking.

1. Write a list of twenty different fashion brands – it does not matter who they are.

   Now decide if you like or dislike these brands and give the reasons for each of your decisions.

2. Develop an electronic trend or mood board. Focus on directions in both colour and style. Brainstorm various themes based upon your research with others.

3. Visit three different fashion retailers of your choice: one multi-brand department store, one chain store and one designer store and also review the websites. What differences or similarities do you see? Consider style, colour, fabric and trims and compare price points. Consider the difference online with instore experience. Analyze all these factors.

4. Visit a current art gallery or museum exhibition. View the exhibits, bearing in mind one or two designer brands that you admire. Then take inspiration from the exhibits to:

   ✗ Think about how some of the information you see may be used in order to help develop inspiration for the brand.

   ✗ Review textile and yarn direction websites online and select fabrics that may inform a collection based on the exhibits, which are in keeping with the philosophy of the brand(s) you admire.

   ✗ Put a colour palette together for a range of products based on those exhibits that you find most interesting.

Product Development

The product development process is essential to the fashion business. In its broadest sense, the term *product development* is used to describe the translation of fashion design concepts, ideas and trends into commercial products. The process begins directly after designers have broken down initial concepts and trends into theme, colour and fabric stories. The next stage is to focus these stories further into specific categories of fashion products and to develop these concepts by turning them into prototype sample garments for review. This chapter examines a generic product development process by identifying the steps followed by mass-market fashion brands, although each fashion retailer will have its own version of the development process, adapted to its target market and customers.

2.1 H&M Collaboration with Giambatissta Valli
Kendall Jenner is seen on the runway at the Valli Loves H&M show in Rome Italy, 2020.

The role of design in business

Different retailers will either elect to buy branded products or develop own-label products; the larger retailers tend to have a mixture of the two. It is important to distinguish between these strategies for the purposes of range planning, which we discuss in more detail later in the chapter.

The designer has a crucial role to develop the right products at the right price. It is essential that fashion retailers employ and train designers with the ability to understand the advantages of adding value at the product development stages. This applies to all segments of the market. It is equally important to be prepared to change the process and adapt it to the ever-changing nature of the market. Designers should have the ability to interact with buyers and merchandisers and be capable of using appropriate skills to justify their ideas for design direction and trends – this is a key dynamic in the fashion retailing sector.

Private label product development

An important part of a retailer's range planning and design strategy is the continuous development of its own brands, often referred to as 'private label'. This kind of product development grew from the need for retailers to buy exactly what they required for their customers and market.

Own-label product development and fashion design has grown to such an extent that sub-brands and designer labels are now included in this category, all of which are still owned completely by the retailer. H&M is well known for its many designer collaborations including Jeremy Scott's Moschino and Margiela. These collaborations began with Karl

Lagerfeld in 2004, although the Balmain's 2015 collection was widely considered to be the most successful. Collaboration is a win-win for luxury brands, as it helps gain enormous exposure and adds profit whilst for a brand such as H&M success hinges on the ability to generate interest and drive customers to purchase often limited editions.

Many retailers have realized that offering private label fashion ranges is a key way to achieve differentiation and gain competitive advantage over regular brands. Private label has been around in fashion for a long time; it means that it is wholly owned, created by the brand and usually sold exclusively by them. Private labels can generally gain higher gross margins than 'other' branded products. Plus, the profit margins for apparel far exceed those of food and household items. Offering a private label apparel range also helps retailers carry greater brand equity when added to the mix with other categories, especially supermarkets. The very nature of private label production means that those retailers have total control over product development and production of the garments in terms of quality, design and pricing – without giving up a margin. Private label fashion has contrasting objectives with smaller marketing budgets compared to large fashion houses and brands. They satisfy a different need and appeal to a different consumer. Luckily, there is a place for both. This strategy is not confined to the mass market but includes luxury retailers such as Matches, which has its own label, Raey, whilst The Outnet (owned by Net a Porter) has its own Iris and Ink label.

2.2 Designer Brand Collaboration
Jeremy Scott at Moschino with the creative director of H&M Ann Sofie Johansson at the launch of their collection.

The fashion business and its retailers have definitely seized opportunities for collaborations, which are not confined to the mass market either. Louis Vuitton and Supreme, Fendi and Fila, Polo Ralph Lauren and Palace, JW Anderson and Converse, Burberry and Vivienne Westwood, Gosha Rubchinskiy and Vetements are some of the more upmarket brand collaborations.

Brands that are brought in as part of a retail range-planning strategy are often intended to fit around the core customer and complement retailers' own labels as a part of the product mix. The trend has been for retailers to increase the proportion of own-label fashion brands, driven by the need to retain control of the design and development process or work with famous designer names to create their own label ranges. All this means that the retailer's product development resource is now extensive and highly skilled, and less likely to rely on suppliers' design capability. Large teams of designers, technologists and support staff, such as pattern cutters, graphics or print designers and administrators, are employed by fashion retailers to design and develop unique, exclusive ranges.

Developing the initial concepts

During the initial concept phase, designers begin by creating sketches showing detailed silhouettes to illustrate the garments in their range. These sketches can be created manually with pen and scanned into a CAD program or created directly using CAD software. The initial sketches are used to begin to shape the number of looks or styles in each story for presentations to buyers.

Mood boards are used to provide an early visual indication of proposed colour direction, fabric and trims and key silhouettes for each look. Designers will use swatches of fabric and scan the fashion press for ideas and clippings to illustrate the boards. In this way, the content of international media publications such as *Vogue* or *Vanity Fair* form part of the planning process for each season.

2.3　Raey Private Label
Freelance fashion writer Tilly Macallister Smith wearing Raey jacket at Paris Fashion week.

These trend boards and the sketches are reviewed, changed and adapted many times to determine the exact direction for the brand or retailer. The final process of range planning will result in full-colour sketches showing all styles and suggested colours and fabrics. Often referred to as 'ways', each style will have a detailed ID or blueprint and a description, which will include full working technical drawings known as garment specification sheets or specifications as a part of a technical pack for manufacturing.

Developing the range plan

After the initial design concept of fabrics, colour and general styling direction have been analyzed, the design, buying and merchandising teams begin the next key stage in the process: range planning. This involves turning the rough ideas and sketches into 'stories' or mini collections. There will usually be several general colour and print themes that may be developed simultaneously. In the range plan the sketches and swatches are grouped together and given names such as 'Sport Luxe ', 'New Neutrals' or 'Boho Chic ' to identify inspiration and, often, lifestyle trends. Within each range there may be up to twelve mini collections or 'drops' of smaller ranges and also featuring special products as part of the early stages. These themed planning boards – which include detailed sketches, as well as colour and fabric at this stage – are used to demonstrate the thought process and direction that the designers believe should be followed.

The short term nature of the fashion industry has revolved around newness and become faster and faster; developing new product at speed has become the norm. It is debatable that the so-named See now Buy Now influence on design houses is an extension of fast fashion influencing upwards to the luxury market.

'Fast Fashion is a result of Planned Obsolescence however this planned obsolescence is when something is made to break. We all need clothing, so once we have clothing there is really no incentive to buy new clothing except to keep up with the latest styles. Fashion is a by-product of planned obsolescence, but so is the quality of clothing. With a mix of the average worker's wages stagnating since the 1990's, and the freedom allowed to manufacturers to import clothing a new problem has developed. Planned obsolescence to the extreme.'
– Ally Frownie, 2018

The product mix

Fashion retailers have rapidly increased the number of collections available during a typical year. Pioneered by companies such as Benetton and Zara, the model in fashion retailing shifted from seasonal purchasing to shorter, rapid bursts of new products. What we know is that fast fashion has evolved from the 'quick response' clothing manufacturing model (which we discuss in more detail in Chapter 4: The Supply Chain). The designers, buyers and merchandisers review the sales history with the design teams, such as good and bad sellers, emerging trends and the performance of their competition in the market. This is often referred to as a 'lessons learnt' stage and it is a crucial part of the range planning process.

Phased product ranges or 'drops of product' in season

Fashion product has become much less seasonal and is one of continual newness, with so-called drops of product and colours and fabrics continually being introduced to customers. This extends from the mass market to luxury brands such as Moncler and Louis Vuitton.

Drops is an increasingly common name for a controlled release of limited edition product, often on a weekly or monthly rhythm. This is faster than the traditional fashion cycle and designed to create consumer excitement with a stream of 'newness'. This concept of regularly drip-feeding product in limited quantities was pioneered in Japan by Hiroshi Fujiwara and popularized by streetwear brands like Supreme, Palace and Nike, who have now adopted the system at retail and online.

The product mix and range-planning process is loosely based upon what is known as the marketing mix (or the 10P's), which is the total offer to customers (see Figure 2.5). Each fashion retailer will adapt these principles to suit their brand in the context of its market. The marketing mix is a useful model to explain the key stages within fashion retail.

The range plan

The range plan is essential for determining product mix. The plan contains complete details of all styles, including the required lead times for each style and how many phases are going to exist within each range. The overall styling direction and theme of each range will usually be determined at this stage. Phases of delivery and drops of new products are timed for each collection, which allows new colour statements and products to be introduced.

The team of designers, buyers and merchandisers will determine the total number of styles required per category of product, such as knitwear or tailoring. They will analyze the proportion and balance of each range, such as quantity of tops versus trousers or daywear versus evening wear (usually there will be more tops than bottoms and more daywear than occasion wear). They will also decide what percentage of each range will be fashion, classic or basics. Finally, they make decisions on types of fabrics and numbers of colours per style, based on trends, availability and suitability. Additionally, the size ranges will be agreed at this stage, such as skirt and trouser lengths for example, or special fits such as petite or tall.

The fashion product critical path

The critical path (CP) identifies the steps that need to take place in order for the products to arrive into the distribution centre on the required date defined by the business and is sometimes known as design to delivery management or a timeline. The CP is the glue that binds the process together. It is designed to list a number of associated tasks, which, when combined with a time duration, will define the length of time it takes to complete a project.

So what makes a critical path critical? It is because the steps involved will determine the total completion time for the fashion product. If one duration time increases, for example trimming or packaging, then either another must decrease to ensure the product is delivered on time or the delivery date gets set back and then you need to consider what the impact of that would be on the business.

Here are the key steps of a fashion critical path (in a very generic sense) and should be adapted by any brand for each of its product ranges.

1. Initial brainstorm of ideas including fabric yarn colour and silhouette
2. Shows/Shopping for inspiration
3. Development trips
4. Previous season performance analysis
5. Plan and forecast all merchandising plans
6. Company present strategy
7. Strategy meeting
8. Develop product
9. Select supplier
10. Produce buying samples
11. Build range
12. Analyze and agree range
13. Sign off product
14. Produce purchase order
15. Undertake fit process
16. Create product and raise purchase order
17. Approve and issue purchase order and update the delivery schedule
18. Agree the delivery dates
19. Purchase order confirmed by supplier
20. Request a pre-production sample
21. Approve a pre-production sample
22. Order is manufactured
23. Request production sample
24. Approve production sample
25. Brand to issue the authority to supplier to deliver
26. Update the purchase order on the delivery schedule
27. Photograph products
28. Product ready to go live on the website
29. Website proofing

Make sure that these steps are followed at each stage. Next is a responsibility assignment matrix, a common tool used in business planning.

Responsible	Who is responsible for actually doing it?
Accountable	Who has authority to approve or disapprove it?
Consulted	Who needs to be consulted?
Informed	Who needs to be kept informed about the task?

In the importance of monitoring the CP it is important to consider the following points: What could go wrong and if it does, what would the impact be? What decisions could you make during the CP stage that you could not make once the product has been delivered?

The ten P's

The four Ps (product, price, place and promotion) were established by Borden in 1965. The model was further extended, known as the extended marketing mix, to include three intangible, service-related elements – people, process and physical evidence – and eventually three more to the now extended 10Ps.

There is also a further model of Cs by Lauterborn, known as The 4Cs (Customer, Cost, Convenience and Communication), which was developed to help us think in terms of customers' concerns more than our own. The thought process here is to go from being business-oriented with the 10Ps and to include the 4Cs in your thought process and tactics to make your brand more customer focused. A balance of both models is probably worth consideration.

2.4 Ralph Lauren Store Bond Street London
Ralph Lauren shows off its 3D technology and celebrates ten years of digital innovation with a display in London.

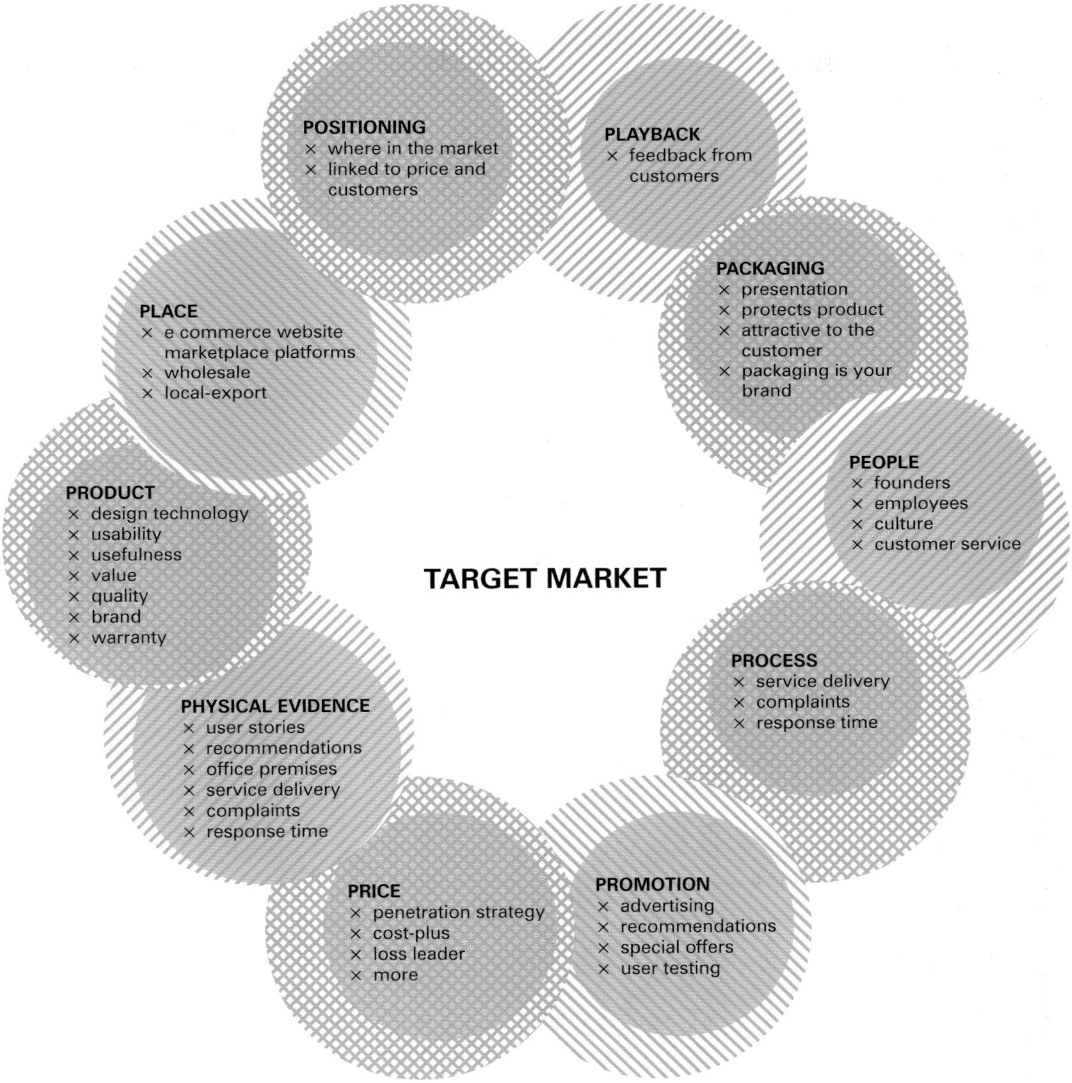

POSITIONING
× where in the market
× linked to price and
customers

PLAYBACK
× feedback from
customers

PACKAGING
× presentation
× protects product
× attractive to the
customer
× packaging is your
brand

PLACE
× e commerce website
marketplace platforms
× wholesale
× local-export

PEOPLE
× founders
× employees
× culture
× customer service

PRODUCT
× design technology
× usability
× usefulness
× value
× quality
× brand
× warranty

TARGET MARKET

PROCESS
× service delivery
× complaints
× response time

PHYSICAL EVIDENCE
× user stories
× recommendations
× office premises
× service delivery
× complaints
× response time

PRICE
× penetration strategy
× cost-plus
× loss leader
× more

PROMOTION
× advertising
× recommendations
× special offers
× user testing

2.5 **The 10 P's**

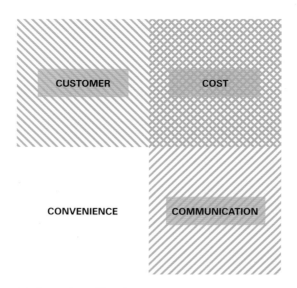

2.6 Lauterborn Model
The 4Cs model encourages you to consider the customer, cost, convenience, and communication.

Basics or core items

Hosiery, T-shirts, denim and lingerie are all examples of basic or core items. It is important to note that these require redesigns and continual seasonal updates, which may include new fabrics, improved fit, colour and new trimmings to coordinate with the fashion look.

There will also be key pieces or must-haves that are added to the basics range each season. The basic product lines are usually safe and best-selling items and must be available all year round, regardless of the season. These are mass market, high volume lines with a higher margin than for fashion items and a low product development cost.

Fashion items

These are the true 'fashion' lines, which demand crucial timing and very limited selling periods. It is impossible to list them here as they are simply 'fashion' and therefore unpredictable. However, it is important to note that garments that are fashion items may in the future become basics or classics, such as the little black dress.

Different product categories have different requirements; for example, in some ranges there must be more basics available as well as fashion items. The balance of each product, phase and range is crucial to the success of product development translation from the design concepts.

2.7 H&M Pop-Up Store
A pop-up H&M store showcasing the Giambattista Valli collaboration of 'Giambattista Valli Loves H&M Cocktail Dinatorie' in Rome, Italy.

2.8 A Primark Store
A range of basic items in volume on display in a Primark Store London.

The range-planning process usually involves a collaboration of the designer, buyer and merchandiser to determine the product mix. This establishes the design details of all styles, the required lead times for each style and the number of phases within each range.

Basic product lines are best-selling, high-volume items that are available all year round, regardless of the season.

Garment specifications: sampling

Once the range-planned styles have been agreed and signed off, the design team will work with the pattern and fabric technologists to perfect the detailed information required in order to proceed to the initial sampling stages.

The garment spec is sent to the relevant manufacturer with clear instructions on how it should look and the type of fabric required for making the sample. A CAD (computer-aided design) sketch and diagram or photograph will be included, along with a mock-up or toile of part, or all, of the entire garment. It is usually dependent upon the size of the company whether or not it has its own sample room facilities. Making samples is an expensive and laborious part of the design process

and each sample will take far longer to make than its mass-produced final version. This is why the range-planning process is so crucial: it is far cheaper, less wasteful and more efficient for retailers and their suppliers to develop mood boards and sketches than excessive sampling of garments.

Many large retailers rely heavily on suppliers to perfect and develop buying samples for them. CAD techniques are used to enable design and buying teams to view multiple colourways and detailing of garments without the need to sample them all; however, it is important to note that this relies on the CAD designer having very good communication as well as design skills.

Garment sampling may occur in-house, depending on the size of the fashion retailer; but more often the retailer will rely on its manufacturers and suppliers.

Toile

A toile is a mock-up used to check the pattern and design of a garment. Different to a sample, it is used at an earlier stage in the design process. The toile may be made in calico or a cheaper version of the required fabric.

2.9 CAD Design
A designer and merchandiser are seen working on CAD designs and planning ranges.

Performance testing

All products developed must pass performance testing requirements. It is usually the responsibility of the supplier to ensure that all products meet, or exceed, the standards required by the retailer. Before finalizing or signing an agreement, it is important that suppliers understand and agree the quality-standard requirements of the retailer. It is normal practice to have both fabric and garments tested before the product is delivered; typically, the testing is done at a third-party testing facility such as Intertek or ITS. At times, the buyers and design team will designate the testing lab. Sometimes the retailer (or buyer) will submit the garments for testing; however, often the buyer will require that the supplier submits the fabric and garments directly to the testing laboratory and then provide them with copies of the test results. Final bulk testing is completed before bulk production of garments commences. Accurate records must be kept by the manufacturer and the retailer in case of any faults or customer complaints. Many retailers also undertake surprise testing on garments after they arrive in the stores. This technique is used to discourage suppliers from submitting garments in bulk that do not match up to the quality approved for final production.

In the fashion business as in any business we have different categories of products and brands within a group when it comes to profitability.

2.10 Zara Store London
Customers entering a large Zara store on Oxford St London stocking basic items and new 'fast fashion'.

The Boston Consulting Group matrix (BCG) is a useful model to explain the different categories of product owned brands from a sales perspective. Following is an example – the list is adapted from Marci Martin, 'What is a BCG Matrix', *Business News Daily*, 27 September 2018'.

Stars: The products that have the best market share and generate the most cash are considered stars.

Example: Zara Denim and Womens basics

Cash cows: Cash cows are the leaders in the marketplace and generate more cash than they consume. These are products that have a high market share, provide the cash required to turn question marks into market leaders, and pay dividends to shareholders. Companies are advised to invest in cash cows to maintain productivity and to 'milk' the gains.

Example: Zara Jackets Dresses Shoes

Dogs: Dogs, or pets as they are sometimes known, are units or products that have a low market share and a low growth rate. They frequently break even, neither earning nor consuming a great deal of cash.

Example: Maternity and Childrens ranges

Question marks: These parts of a business have high growth prospects but a low market share. They consume a lot of cash but bring little in return.

2.11 At Work in a Fashion Design Studio
A fashion technologist at work in her studio checking the fit and quality of the latest collection.

Question marks, also known as problem children, lose money but have the potential to turn into stars.

Example: Pull & Bear, Bershka

Specialist fabrics: Some garments will require additional testing, such as items that claim to be flame retardant, water-resistant, anti-bacterial, and so on. So-called 'smart' fabrics are used for sport and other performance activities, which need to be fit for purpose; Teflon-coated, breathable and water-repellent fabrics require rigorous testing before use. Even simple products, such as a T-shirt jersey, for example, require certain dyes to withstand washing and to limit the shrinkage of fabric. Children's apparel requires additional product safety testing. Recycled, reused and repurposed materials are another type of specialist fabric considered by designers and are now a fundamental choice as part of the product development process as textiles manufacturers innovate and blend technology with sustainability. See Chapter 4: Supply Chain, page 93.

By the time it reaches the mass-production stage, each garment style will have been technically engineered in order to be as cost-effective and aesthetically pleasing as possible, reflecting the original model and ideas of the designer.

Interview
Steven Tai, Designer and founder of steventai

With a BA in Fashion Design from London's Central St Martins, Steven has worked at design houses including Viktor & Rolf and Stella McCartney before starting his own label, steventai, in 2012.

The steventai womenswear brand is progressive, technically detailed and luxurious and encourages a relaxed tomboy look that defies mainstream trends. By celebrating the feeling of ease, steventai collections often reference sportswear and are loose fitted. This casual comfort is then elevated with innovative technological developments on fabrics that create a unique blend of luxury and comfort.

Tell us a little bit about yourself.

I studied for a business degree in Canada and then did a BA in women's fashion design at Central St Martins. I was very interested in design but never thought I would have my own label. I interned at Stella McCartney after graduation and when I was there I applied to a competition in France called the Hyères Fashion Festival which has run for twenty-seven years with amazing alumni of juries and winners. Previous juries included Galliano and Lacroix and the year I was a finalist, the judge was Yohji Yamamoto. So it was huge honour to present my work in front of such a legend. It was also there, I won the first ever Chloé Award. It was because of that Mercedes Benz invited me to do a show in Berlin.

Because of that experience this made me want to set up my own brand, but I resisted initially as I thought many people didn't know what they were doing by setting up a brand right after graduation. So, I expanded my graduate collection to a full collection and from there people

became interested. I had orders and realized that people would kill for an opportunity like this, so I thought if I didn't do it then I might miss the chance, so I took the plunge and set up the brand.

What is your design and style philosophy?

Basically, my label is always a reflection of who I am and my experiences that have highlighted key moments in my life. That is something I learned at St Martins. It is always important to be authentic to your own history to create the most personal work.

For me, my mum has always been a significant influence. She is a real 'boss lady' that I have been around all my life and looking back, I realize I have always been surrounded by powerful women. When I was a kid, I used to go shopping with mom and as she was not petite, I remembered she struggled to find clothes that fitted her well. I felt it was such a shame that this was not an enjoyable or pleasurable experience for her.

So, because of this, I wanted to make clothes that were not form-fitting and quite powerful. My mom also never wears dresses or skirts which is why our looks are always so separates and trousers driven.

I think this childhood experience merged with my teenage years where I was an immigrant from Macau growing up in Canada. There, I felt that I never quite fitted in and I ended up as part of a group of in-betweeners in high school. We were all very geeky but so different in terms of personalities. We were very confident about who we were and I wanted the brand to reflect that energy, where we embrace something non-confirmative and not often considered 'beautiful'.

Who is your customer in your head?

The brand is six years old – so now I have a much better understanding of who she is and who our customer is: she is 20–35 and she works in a creative industry. Over the last couple of seasons, I have tried to grow the customers up a bit.

At its core, our customer is someone who never quite fitted in but is happy with herself. She doesn't need to subscribe to fashion's pressure to look or dress a certain way to have appeal, rather she believes in herself despite being completely aware of her faults, and rather walks to her own off-beat drum.

What is great style in your view?

I struggle with that; I think great style is when someone can express succinctly who they are through dress. It is hard for me to say which is the best style; in my view, it is about the person who emulates their attitude or perspective on life. Whereas, I think design is about the garment itself, which can help create the style. Design is the ingredient and style is the dish!

Which other designers or contemporaries do you admire?

There are such a lot of designers that I admire and I tend to think very highly of everyone. But I really admire brands like A.W.A.K.E. by Natalia Alaverdian, I also love Alex Mullins and Cecile Branson, but there are so many designers doing great things out there. In terms of bigger brands and names – Undercover is my favourite brand of all time.

Where does your main source of inspiration come from?

I think it comes from daily life and the people around me. I think I pick up on their attitudes and things that they are experiencing.

Which commercial mass-market retailers do you regard as doing a good job with product development?

At a high street level, the H&M group, which includes their other brands such as Monki, COS, ARKET, and other stores. I really think that the H&M group is pretty amazing to manage opening all of these brands. They may not be the most sustainable but they are really skilled at slicing that pie so finely and taking a big bite!

What are your thoughts on the range-planning process?

I think the range-planning process is extremely important. We look through previous season's sales figures and it informs us what worked well and what didn't with our clients.

The most interesting thing about looking at previous sales records is that you can actually systematically discover whether we are making too many skirts when we should be doing more shirts, etc. It is a bit like an experiment and each season offers a chance of fine-tuning the range plan.

How do you research your customers?
Now I am doing more of this research than before as in the beginning, I was spending all my time figuring out how to run a business. We didn't really have the luxury to do too much research as it takes a lot of time and energy and we are a very small team. Thanks to the fact that because we are opening an online store, I have been forced to delve deep into social media. Which is helping us to learn about customers, for example, when do they visit our page, what items are they looking at, what age group are they, and where they are based.

What is a typical day for you in the design studio?
I don't think there is one – this is a part of the joy of having my own business in that I am never bored. I might have a meeting or two in the morning but as I work with Asia's factory very closely, I have to check 'Wechat' and 'Whatsapp' the minute I wake up. Normally I will be working on these messages on the way to work or meeting. When I arrive in the studio I then make sure the interns are okay, answering any questions and fitting issues whilst checking e-mails constantly, contacting suppliers and researching into anything I am currently interested in.

Recently it has been a bit more of a crazy schedule as Fashion Week is coming up. I would normally work till 9 or 10 p.m. in the office, go home, eat and then by 12 midnight the messages are coming in from Asia again so I can sometimes end up working around the clock.

Do you use Trend Forecasting Sites services?
No, not at all. We put our own trend services together. I think these bought-in services are more relevant for larger size business; in the mass market you are investing heavily on advertising and grabbing mass attention. So they have to respond to trends much more quickly. For us, I think it is more about what we love and want to create in the moment, and that is our trend.

Case Study

MATCHESFASHION.COM

(This case study was written by the author and taken from an interview with Hannah Fillis.)

MATCHESFASHION began thirty years ago, with its first physical store opening in Wimbledon by the founders Tom and Ruth Chapman who went on to open several other stores in London in locations such as Notting Hill, Marylebone and Richmond. Seeing the expansion of online retail, twenty years on, the e-commerce arm was launched as MATCHESFASHION.COM. This was not intended to replace physical stores, but to complement them as a separate element, providing online storytelling content to go with the fashion buying and collections. This is when Ulrich Jerome (who is now CEO) was taken on to strengthen the digital side of the business. After thirty years, Tom and Ruth Chapman stepped down from running the businesss, but MATCHESFASHION.COM continued with the same ethos as when the Chapmans first set the business up. The backstory of the brand remains an important element to the company, in part to illustrate to customers why the brands sold are as relevant, different and important as they were from their Wimbledon store beginnings.

Townhouse store 5 Carlos Place, London
The original Townhouse store was in Marylebone, but moved to a larger space in Mayfair which spans across five floors. It is a store open to everyone, with art installations changing every couple of weeks to further support the experiential element of the retailer. The Townhouse has two floors devoted exclusively to personal shopping suites and can provide everything in a customer's private wishlist to be ready and waiting for them when they arrive.

As well as the art installations the Townhouse store holds many events for the fashion industry, such as seasonal press days and brand launches, many of which are open for anyone to attend by signing up to the event via their website. A variety of activities are held, from intimate music events to pottery classes, the latter of which was for a launch of a ceramic jewellery and homeware brand. The brand has also held 'in conversation' with interviews with designers, photographers and other fashion and artistic creatives including Molly Goddard speaking about her unique design process as well as Tommy Ton and Andrea Tsao. These events were hosted by Highsnobiety's editor-at-large, Christopher Morency and Matches' buying director Natalie Kingham.

Vision statement

MATCHESFASHION.COM's 'vision' is paramount and internally everything the business does links back to its brand DNA and goal, which is 'to be the most personal luxury shopping experience service in the world', according to Hannah Fillis.

When MATCHESFASHION.COM is creating or considering any new project it always considers 'the vision' and uses it to inform the decision-making process to ensure each activity fits with its ethos, asking 'how might this improve service for customers?'. Once a year MATCHESFASHION.COM holds a company-wide event, which begins by reviewing its vision and setting the scene with this important statement.

A global luxury success story

There are a couple of specific and unique elements including new designers and exclusive collaborations with global brands which have contributed to the success of MATCHESFASHION.COM. These important steps are linked to creating a point of difference in the way buying teams choose products and select new brands that are unique, exclusive and different to the competitors.

New designers

MATCHESFASHION.COM is well known for championing and supporting new young designer brands and often giving them their first platform, such as Vetements and Halpern. Some of its new designers have become successful well-known brands and have then created exclusive specially commissioned pieces and collections for MATCHESFASHION.COM such as Christopher Kane and Molly Goddard. To support this strategy, the buying team works very closely with all designer brands to curate and edit the collection and create a partnership. This strategy is well known across the industry as a 'calling card' of MATCHESFASHION.COM.

Global brands

The buyers also work closely with global luxury brands such as Prada, Gucci and Yves Saint Laurent who have all gone on to create exclusive collections for MATCHESFASHION.COM.

It is important to highlight that the integration of the storytelling element is crucial in supporting such partnerships through all channels – editorial, social media and e-mail content – to keep everything relevant. These long-term partnerships last season after season and can take 6–12 months to create the storytelling content that supports these partnerships. It is not just a case of 'here is a new brand'; rather the collection is showcased and promoted in a unique and original manner.

2.12 **Molly Goddard Runway Show London**
A model walks the runway at the Molly Goddard show during London Fashion Week September 2019 in London, UK.

When MATCHESFASHION.COM opened the Townhouse at 5 Carlos Place an exclusive partnership and promotional launch was developed with Prada who created a 'Neon' collection using iconic shapes and designs. Simultaneously, MATCHESFASHION.COM was also working on an in-store installation with the designer Robert Storey. As Prada is such a playful brand, together they created lots of fun elements such as the Prada-branded pinball machines and vending machines with neon lights. The result was a launch that matched the Prada brand perfectly, made possible because of the close relationship developed with MATCHESFASHION.COM.

There was also unique artwork created for the website, for example, a launch of the digital 'Prada World', as part of the Prada launch, consisting of six illustrated worlds created by different artists. Each 'world' was 'unlocked' on the website to coincide as each Prada collection 'dropped' in stores and online. The models on the website were an important feature of the animation theme and a different version of the animation was used in the social media campaigns to generate new content and interest at each interaction with customers. The entire campaign was creatively very different to the way Prada had worked with any other retailer which further helped to position MATCHESFASHION.COM as a unique Prada partner.

Brand selection process and curating the collections

The marketing teams travel with the buyers who condense and share information with the rest of the business to invest in x woman, x brand, x product and key looks for the seasons ahead. The marketing team's role is to show how brands and designers are important for the next season and consider carefully what has been bought so they can create appropriate marketing strategies. The next step is to create a marketing campaign and events that highlight the key partnerships, such as the preceding Prada example, condensed into in-depth planning documents as part of the overall marketing and buying strategy.

The buying process and promotions are intrinsically linked; however, it is important to note that the buyers do not buy into market trends. MATCHESFASHION.COM has six women's profiles it considers and 'buys' for (but it is important to note that the same customer can be all six of these women at different times). This is dependent on activities and so there is a crossover of the profiles all rolled into one customer as they can change from season to season. If a brand does not fit with the six women's profiles and their needs then a collection may not be bought.

Some examples of these profiles include:

> **The Curator** – she is all about fabric and textiles
>
> **The Minimalist** – she has a very pared look with a clean colour palette
>
> **The Fashion Pioneer** – she is the first person to have the look or product

2.13 **Street Style: A Neon Prada Bag**
Aylin Koenig is seen with a Neon Prada bag in Hamburg, Germany.

2.14 MATCHESFASHION.COM
Laurel (R) attends the MATCHESFASHION.COM Moncler X Richard Quinn launch at 5 Carlos Place.

2.15 The Cultivist X MATCHESFASHION.COM Event
This is a view of the space during The Cultivist x MatchesFashion.com at The Bazaar in New York City.

2.16 Attendees at MATCHESFASHION.COM Event
Sita Abellan and Miranda Makaroff attend the MATCHESFASHION.COM Moncler X Richard Quinn launch at 5 Carlos Place.

When considering the product and brand mix and editing the collections at MATCHESFASHION.COM these six multifaceted customer profiles are considered carefully as an important aspect of the buying decision-making process. MATCHESFASHION.COM buyers constantly scout out younger designer brands; they are on the road 80 percent of the year reviewing collections and visiting showrooms and are very open to newness. For example, Fillis recalled that on one occasion buyers were approached in a hotel by a young designer to visit her showroom, which the buyers loved and went on to purchase the collection. Designers also send products to the buying team who, as discussed earlier, is very proactive about establishing new relationships with designers and brands. MATCHESFASHION.COM works equally closely with more well-known brands and reviews these names regularly as part of the selection process.

As an example of this, it has begun stocking the fashion label of Katharine Hamnett. This is partly because MATCHESFASHION.COM understands the importance of sustainability and KH obviously fits with this ethos as a leading brand with a reputation in this important field.

Digital and physical marketing
MATCHESFASHION.COM has several different strands of marketing to current customers using e-mail, physical mail, their website, and of course social media.

Digital marketing is carefully considered by region and the marketing strategy is adapted and applied to match,

for example in some markets MATCHESFASHION.COM e-mail is king and for other regions all shopping is done via the app. So it is important to make sure not to just focus on one channel, but use all relevant platforms and tailor its digital marketing strategies to reach all global customers. Within acquisition MATCHESFASHION.COM uses social media platforms as communcation tools and follows brands who it sees as being potential future customers.

Pay-per-click adverts (PPC) on social media are another method used to reach new customers. One of the newer channels used are affiliates – other websites – as another element of digital marketing at MATCHESFASHION.COM as well as influencers who have become a social media phenomenom. MATCHESFASHION.COM has large followings of key opinion leaders (KOLs); these influencers are extremely engaged and link with the brand aesthetic so the relationships are very organic. As they represent the brand aesthetic on a global scale, it is important to reach the influencer's audience, too, as another layer of communications.

It is the style of the influencer that is important, for example, MATCHESFASHION.COM recently did a partnership at Salon de Mobile show in Paris (homeware). This was advertised as 'A week at Salon de Mobile with an artist', who of course was wearing MATCHESFASHION.COM and sharing information about the fair. Events are yet another channel of marketing communications; it is important to note that no activity is carried out 'en masse' but is instead carefully selected region by region.

Content creation

There are several important factors when planning content for the site and at the start of the year all planned events are strategically prioritized into large scale events, key partnerships and moments. For example, it could be very simple to ensure upcoming collections may fit into the next vacation season or Christmas gifting, which usually starts at the end of October. However, having deliveries and stock availability is what is paramount, and each week every element of the promotions are aligned with deliveries and the marketing and promotions team ensure features coincide with stock availability. For example, if this is an event at 5 Carlos Place it is not just the event, but having the correct products alongside, say, a Louboutin exclusive product launch – everything is carefully thought through by coordinating marketing, retail and PR and stock.

RAEY private label

RAEY is a completely separate in-house private label brand from the MATCHESFASHION.COM's stand-alone store in Notting Hill London. RAEY was created after Ruth Chapman felt there was a gap in women's wardrobes for modern stylish basics, such as a cashmere roll neck that would last season to season. When the brand was launched, Rachel Proud was appointed as the Creative Director and the strategy for RAEY was that it would operate separately to MATCHESFASHION.COM.

It is important to point out that RAEY is positioned as an exclusive brand and separate from the MATCHESFASHION.COM buying team. The brand team at RAEY has its own buying strategy and moved from seasonal collections to regular 'drops' all year round. This drop model means there are regular uploads of products online every 4–6 weeks in addition to RAEY's standalone offices, social media accounts and website. RAEY.COM acts as an independent brand but shares exclusive links to MATCHESFASHION.COM.

Personalization and service

MATCHESFASHION.COM takes customer service very seriously and has a shipping programme called 'On the Dot' which guarantees delivery within 90 minutes in London, and same day delivery in other parts of the UK and USA.

Packaging is very important as part of the delivery and service experience, and every last detail is considered by MATCHESFASHION.COM, which is well known for its recognisable iconic marble boxes carefully constructed with magnetic fastenings. The packages are not only functional, but collectable, encased in beautiful tissue paper. The aim is to create a beautiful 'unboxing' moment for customers, with each package including a personalized note from the person who packed it.

The private shopping team at Carlos Place allows customers to book an appointment at short notice and then gathers all products they are interested in ready for when the customer walks in. This is another aspect of MATCHESFASHION. COM taking service to the next level. E-mail communication is equally personalized, with the customer's designer preferences noted. There is a CURATOR loyalty programme which is open to every customer with different levels of rewards. These are not just monetary rewards, there are other imaginitive experiences awarded to customers on a very personal level, such as a dedicated MATCHESFASHION.COM contact, birthday and seasonal rewards linked to personal taste, and exclusive access to events and one-off experiences. MATCHESFASHION.COM is one of the first luxury retailers to offer such a programme.

International events

Travel is an important element for the events teams, with the company's largest market being in the USA and the UK as their second. The company has held an LA partnership in the Art Fair Frieze and had a space there, so that current and new customers could visit. It created a 'pop-up' and private shopping space that held various events including music over the four days. These events included interviews with Cher Coulter, a celebrity stylist in LA, and Laura from Rodarte talking about red carpet style, with music from Suki Waterhouse. MATCHESFASHION.COM also holds global events on a smaller scale, such as a private dinner in Dubai where it took designer Michael Halpern to meet press and customers there.

Global collections

MATCHESFASHION.COM recognizes it has a global audience and collections are bought for all regions. Although the same applies to marketing, this strategy works because of the level of personalisation that is built into its customer service.

Point of difference

The quality and how and where clothes are made is so essential to MATCHESFASHION.COM that it has a separate part of the website dedicated to this topic and talks to all of its brands and designers about their environmental footprint and the impact of the entire supply chain including the workforce. Hannah Fillis expresses, 'It is so important to retailers and brands to be very clear about their POD and clear about what they are designing and who they are designing it for', proving that this topic is no longer left to just a handful of sustainable brands. MATCHESFASHION. COM proactively talks to brands about this as it realizes it is very important to its customers. Fillis talks about how customers are increasingly 'moving away from buying just for the sake of buying, [and] want to keep products and buy quality', preferring instead to 'have one good t-shirt rather than 5 cheap ones.'

Chapter summary

This chapter has explored the concept of product development within a fashion retail business and the process of range planning. We have seen that most large-scale retailers and high-street brands develop ranges in-house in order to control the process. In addition, we have discussed how retailers develop the product and marketing mix to suit their customers' needs and to stay ahead of the competition.

Questions and discussion points

We have examined the generic product development process and the process of range planning. Consider the following questions in connection with fashion retail and your understanding of Chapter 2:

1. Identify the different types of products in similar categories from different fashion retail stores – try to ascertain bought-in brands and own labels. What key differences do you see?

2. Which retailers that develop own labels/ranges/lines do you regard as fashionable? Explain why.

3. How well do you think mass market retailers present key trends to customers both online and instore? Discuss.

4. Which fashion brands do you perceive as being innovative and which do you see as not? Why?

5. How well do you think fashion retailers interpret catwalk and general trends? Which fashion retailers do you perceive as doing this most effectively?

Exercises

Fashion retailers spend a great deal of time range planning, which is not always obvious to the public at large. Take some time to examine a variety of fashion retailers and the products on offer. These exercises are designed to make you think like a commercial designer or fashion buyer and understand this key part in the process.

1. Visit a fashion retailer of your choice (both online and offline) and identify how many colour stories or themes are available. What do you think is the specific design direction and overall styling theme of each range? Review the number of styles on display and identify different types of products that you consider to be core, fashion or key items.

2. Think about a key trend that you have identified and consider how different fashion retailers or fashion brands have interpreted this. Compare and contrast retailers' own brands and review key differences or similarities.

3. Take a close look at fabric and detail: what are the emerging themes and similarities do you see from retailer to retailer?

   Examine fabric construction and washing instructions in a variety of stores; again, do these vary by retailer or brand?

4. Develop your understanding of technical innovation within fashion retail. Visit a major sportswear brand such as Nike or Adidas and identify some smart or specially finished products. Identify any promotional swing tags that explain the key benefits to customers.

Retail Strategy

3

Shopping, or 'retail therapy', is a recognizable global leisure activity. Retailers compete with each other by creating interesting and exciting shopping and leisure environments dedicated to attracting and retaining customers. This retail environment encompasses online as well as offline and creating an 'experience' through content as well as a great product is paramount in the digital worlds. In Chapter 2 we discussed product, one of the 10 P's of the marketing mix (see page 43). This chapter reviews position, place, price and people as part of retail strategy. It explores the strategies used by retailers to deliver clothing to customers across the different retail formats.

**3.1 MATCHESFASHION.COM
& Prada Celebrate the Launch
of 5 Carlos Place**
Roksanda Ilincic attends as
Matchesfashion.com and
Prada celebrate the launch
of the Townhouse at 5 Carlos
Place London and their
exclusive collaboration.

3.2 Visual Merchandising
Here we can see a visual merchandising team dressing mannequins in a shop window.

Defining retail strategy

Johnson and Scholes (2012) defined strategy as 'the direction and scope of an organization over the long-term: which achieves advantage for the organization through its configuration of resources within a challenging environment, to meet the needs of markets and to fulfil stakeholder expectations.'

There are two major components to marketing and retail strategy: how the business will address the increasingly competitive marketplace; and how it intends to implement and support its day-to-day operations. It is essential to identify the main competition and to understand strengths and weaknesses alongside those of the competition, which will help to determine retail strategy and position in the market. It is also essential to analyze the business, its competitors and the external environment: macro factors can positively or negatively impact the industry and the market growth potential of the product or service. In addition, key components for strategic analysis include a review of product, price, market position, strength and predictability. A regular review of the strength and viability of fashion products and the provision of customer service development programmes will heavily influence the direction of any retail strategy.

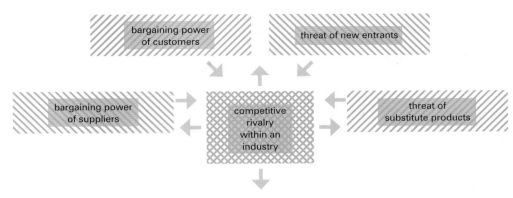

Porter's five forces analysis

3.3 The Five Forces Model, Michael Porter

In his book *Competitive Advantage* Michael Porter developed the Five Forces framework as a technique for understanding and examining the level of power and competitiveness in business. It is a useful tool for analyzing the strength of competitive advantage.

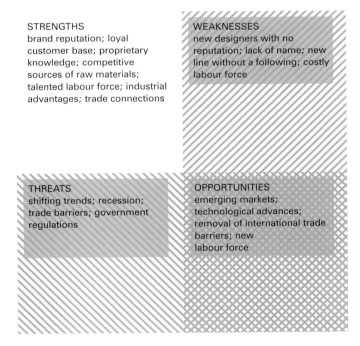

STRENGTHS
brand reputation; loyal customer base; proprietary knowledge; competitive sources of raw materials; talented labour force; industrial advantages; trade connections

WEAKNESSES
new designers with no reputation; lack of name; new line without a following; costly labour force

THREATS
shifting trends; recession; trade barriers; government regulations

OPPORTUNITIES
emerging markets; technological advances; removal of international trade barriers; new labour force

3.4 SWOT Diagram Micro Business Factors

SWOT stands for strengths, weaknesses, opportunities and threats. An honest appraisal of the strengths and weaknesses of the fashion business is a critical factor in the development of its retail strategy. SWOT is an important part of any institutional analysis, usually conducted in conjunction with a PESTEL analysis, see Figure 3.5.

PESTEL framework

We looked at the PESTEL framework in Chapter 1 (see page 18) in the context of trends and forecasting. Retailers use this model to analyze their environment and competition.

Macro factors

Macro factors are wider, external forces; a good example of a macro factor is an economic recession, which has a negative impact upon consumer spending and behaviour in general.

Political: this could be a country introducing changes to import duty.

Economic: recession or boom can affect spending.

Sociological: longer life expectancy means an older population, which in turn affects the products required.

Technological: customer demand for instant information means an increase in the use of marketing tools such as social media.

Environmental: an eco or green and organic movement in textiles.

Legal: changes in copyright law can influence fashion retailers' ability to manufacture certain products.

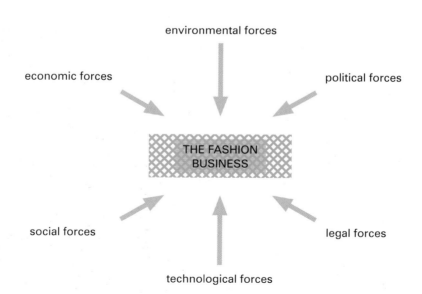

3.5 Macro Factors PESTEL Diagram

There are many factors in the macro-environment that will affect the decision-making process within any industry. To help analyze these factors, retailers can categorize them using the PESTEL model, which is a useful tool in retail strategy.

Implementing retail strategy

Every retail strategy must engage with the philosophy of the company or brand. From retail strategy a fashion business will develop a marketing strategy or plan in order to present the offer in the most effective way and by using the most suitable and efficient retail formats available. It is the brand 'DNA', which is captured in the shopping experience to attract and inspire customers.

According to McKinsey: 'Today's consumer is offered so much choice; as such, the combination of new and innovative store environments and great products is vital to ensure a successful retail strategy. Implementing strategy requires continual review and benchmarking against the competition and analysis of the market environment whilst ensuring that it responds to customers' requirements. Those 20 "super winners," led by Inditex (owner of Zara), Nike and LVMH, account for 97 percent of total industry value created, compared to 70 percent in 2010. The super winners also take the lion's share of industry profits. Other super winners by their calculations include Hermes, Richemont, Kering, Pandora, Luxottica, Michael Kors and Burberry in premium/luxury; Adidas, LBrands, U.K. retailer Next, Vanity Fair Corp, Gap and Hanes Brands in mid-market; and TJMaxx X, H&M, Fast Retailing (Uniqlo) in value. . . ' (McKinsey, 2019, pg. 24).

3.6 UNIQLO STORE, CHINA
Here we see a UNIQLO store in Tianjin, China. UNIQLO has potential to be the world's largest retailer, boasting over 300 stores in China.

Porter's strategies

Porter (1986) identified three generic strategies that can be used to identify the type of retail strategy implemented across different fashion businesses. Each retail strategy is concerned with creating competitive advantage within market position.

× *Overall cost leadership.* Low-cost, high-volume retailers tend to follow this strategy, for example, Primark, Forever 21 and Target. Companies such as this rely on cost leadership for competitive advantage.

× *Differentiation.* Variety and department stores are experts in brand layering and differentiation within their ranges to attract different parts of the market.

× *Focus.* This is very much a niche market strategy, focusing on craftsmanship and a particular product or a category. Luxury brands use a focus strategy, for example, Louis Vuitton, Gucci and Hermès.

UK retailer brand Boden satisfies customer needs by providing good quality goods in specialist fabrics and prints in such a way as to differentiate itself from the competition. This combination of focus and differentiation is a major contributor to its success in maintaining competitive advantage. It is a brand that began as a catalogue and has become an online success; it has now moved into physical stores including John Lewis stores in the UK.

> 'If you look at the best retailers out there they are constantly reinventing themselves.'
> – Burnes, 2009

3.7 Boden Fashion
Here we see the Editor-in-chief of Tank magazine, Caroline Issa, wearing a Boden skirt, at London Fashion Week.

The marketing mix: position

Fashion retailing is a dynamic and fluid business and strategy needs to reflect this: creating a competitive advantage in a market sector is an essential part of maintaining the necessary level of interest.

Identifying market position enables a company to determine its strategy and direction in order to present and maintain a strong recognizable brand image and identity to customers. Analysis of market position involves a lot of detail, such as cost control, infrastructure, cost of materials, economies of scale, management skills, availability of personnel and compatibility of manufacturing resources. A fashion retailing strategy should highlight the way in which the business may construct entry barriers to the competition. These can include high switching costs, gaining substantial benefit from economies of scale via sourcing policies; creating exclusive access to distribution channels to prevent others from using them; and the ability to clearly differentiate products. This is linked to the retailer's ability to buy in bulk and volume and to work with suppliers effectively to create advantages.

Retail positioning

Today's customers have a huge amount of choice; it is vital for a fashion business to identify and maintain market position as part of its retail strategy.

Another important factor to consider is the longevity of fashion products and market position. This is determined by the potential for competitive imitation, the ability to maintain high or low prices and the potential to plan for inevitable fashion product obsolescence. Crucial as part of its competitiveness and positioning is the financial viability and profitability of the business. This will enable it to take key risks and make critical business decisions without too much influence from investors, suppliers and banks.

Obsolescence

An object, service or practice that is no longer wanted goes through the state of obsolescence; it applies to anything that goes 'out of fashion'. According to Mike Easey, the development process for 'the apparel products associated with frequent changes in customer lifestyle and requirements, and that highly rely on fashion marketing, is considered as a planned obsolescence' (Easey, 2002).

Economies of scale

The term 'economies of scale' is used to refer to the fall in the average cost per unit as the scale of output (such as the size of the company or its manufacturing capabilities) increases.

The marketing mix: place

Competition has never been fiercer in international fashion retail, yet there are more opportunities than ever for fashion retailers to obtain and keep new customers. Thanks to the Internet and mobile apps, customers can shop 24/7 if they wish. It is this complexity and dynamism that keeps fashion businesses moving and evolving, much like fashion itself. In addition to retail format, the retailer's location adds another dimension to the marketing offer.

Some retailers will own or rent their own stores whilst others will use different methods to expand strategy and create the most appropriate and interesting retail formats. Many fashion retailers are now using a multi-channel retail strategy to create brand equity. Innovative retail formats, such as pop-up shops, or events and members-only discount e-tailing, add to the complexity of location.

Concessions

Often referred to as a 'shop within a shop', concessions are generally located within large department or variety stores. Many designer brands will use this retail method. One retailer is effectively leasing space to another, which can be a flexible way of testing the market and making use of the retailer's buying and selling expertise. It also means lower investment for the brand and there are potentially higher levels of customer footfall.

Many fashion retailers now use a variety of formats to create brand equity. Luxury retail platform Farfetch has a portfolio of brands as well as international brands that are either bought in or available through in-store concessions.

Franchises

A franchise strategy is often used by retailers who wish to internationalize because it involves low investment: the franchisee has the relevant local knowledge and invests in buying the stock, staffing the store and paying the rent. It means the franchisee can trade under a recognizable, well-known brand and benefit from national or international advertising campaigns. This strategy is often used by own brand retailers, such as Ted Baker and Superdry.

Licensing

A good way for a brand to promote and expand is by selling licences to use its brand name and manufacture products; it is a market penetration technique used by many designer brands. However, it is important to monitor and police the products to ensure they remain true to the brand image. Both Burberry and Gucci have famously fallen foul in the past of over-licensing their products, and had to then carry out a costly and time-consuming repositioning strategy.

Footfall

The number of people visiting a shop or a chain of shops in a period of time is called its footfall. This term is used for online visits too and is an indicator of the reach a retailer has, but it needs to be converted into sales and this is not guaranteed to happen. Many retailers have struggled to turn high footfall into sales.

3.8 Levi's Store
Pedestrians walk past a Flagship Levi's store in Midtown Manhattan, New York.

Online retail

Advances in technology have contributed to the huge growth in online retail, which enables consumers to shop 24/7. The advent of e-tailing has enabled brands to establish a global presence and create yet another competitive edge, a strategy that many fashion brands are now striving for in order to grow market share and increase brand equity.

Designer outlets

In recent years there has been a big increase in the number of large-scale retail outlets, which originated in the USA and have spread to Europe and Asia. Some of these outlet malls are used by designers to distribute out-of-season goods and excess stock. Brands such as Hugo Boss, Max Mara, Jil Sander, and Ralph Lauren are just some of the names that use this retail method to generate lucrative sales revenue. Bicester Village in the UK is one of the largest owners and leasing agents of such designer outlets; FoxTown outside Milan Italy is another such example. Important to note is that 'Made for Outlet' products can be found here. These are

often classic end-of-line products made in cheaper fabric from the 'regular' ranges such as polo shirts, socks and accessories and not just discounted main ranges and excess stocks.

Online discount outlets/clubs

An online version of the outlet store is the members-only designer discounter, such as Gilt Groupe, Vente-Privee, Cocosa and Brand Alley and Zalando or Zalora. These e-tailers all operate in a similar way, offering virtual sample sales with limited availability. Members are e-mailed with the latest offers and given a time limit to make purchases. These retail outlets offer a safety net to brands and designers, enabling them to move excess stock and expensive samples. US company Gilt Groupe saw an opportunity to provide luxury and value to consumers through viral marketing and time-limited sales. It sells brands such as Rodarte, Derek Lam and Christian Louboutin. The company profited during an economic downturn and now has over two million members.

Pop-up shops

Pop-up shops, also known as 'guerilla' stores, have become an accepted way of testing a new location or market over recent years. The concept of the pop-up store is to trial new or well-known brands within a temporary shop outlet. In times of recession, they proved to be a winning low-risk format for many brands.

Newer Retail Models

As many traditional retailers struggle to attract customers and shrink their store networks, a new generation of more nimble digital players is seeing increased opportunity in physical retail with offline activity from born-digital retailers such as Rent the Runway (who have a collaboration with Neiman Marcus) and Bonobos.

Vintage and other resale retail models

In addition to rentals, vintage and collectables are becoming increasingly the norm with everything from accessories to clothing. Online retailers such as Vestiare and The Real Real are key examples. As sustainability continues to increase its footprint such retail models are likely to increase. China plays an important part in the internationalization process of Western brands within the luxury sector, with Louis Vuitton, Gucci and other major names as well as high-street names such as Zara, Uniqlo and H&M prevalent in most cities.

Retail internationalization – 'born global'

Many fashion retailers are international and many others continually try to create a global presence as a part of long-term strategy, but the digital environment means it is easy to be 'born global' as a brand and sell directly to consumers.

Historically, the most successful retailers and fashion brands had sought to maximize global presence through international partnerships, which enabled access to local knowledge and an understanding of local culture, language and taste. This has been made much easier through the use of platforms and marketplace retail formats. Evolving and maturing new markets created new sophisticated and demanding customers

and has enabled fashion retailers to expand. Examples of these include Brazil, China, Russia and India as well as Eastern Europe and the Middle East. It is widely acknowledged that the Chinese market matured very quickly. However, it is far from easy to establish a global presence even via online and it may take years to find the correct partner and format. It is essential that fashion retailers who pursue an international strategy first understand the local market and ensure that the offer is relevant. It may be necessary to adapt and change the mix or offer to fit in with regional and cultural requirements. Well-established global brands such as Uniqlo, Nike and H&M have stores around the world, tailoring the product offering and store environment according to the customers and market of each region whilst creating a unified approach to the brand. A mixture of science and art creates success here.

The marketing mix: price

Price is an essential part of retail strategy. A pricing strategy can help to determine the speed at which a company achieves its marketing objectives. A low price strategy is used to build sales via volume, as used by retailers such as Primark in the UK and Forever 21 in the USA. A higher price strategy is used by companies selling high-quality products, such as the luxury brand Louis Vuitton. Whatever the strategy, the price levels should be set in conjunction with the type of fashion product and be appropriate to market position.

It is important for retailers to work closely with suppliers and manufacturers in order to establish price and profit margins – the retail selling price (RSP). This will ensure that objectives are achieved and that all parties involved are satisfied: this will, of course, include the customer and the price they are willing to pay, as well as the requirements of the retailer and the supplier. All parties must cover their overheads and make a profit to retain sustainability in the long term.

Most fashion retailers use price promotions, sales and special offers as part of a pricing strategy. These are usually planned in the budget setting process at the start of each season and accounted for by buying and merchandising teams.

Luxury brands use a higher price strategy, which is set in conjunction with fashion product type: exclusive, often limited edition, top-quality garments. The pricing strategy should be appropriate to the brand's market position.

Price matrix

Different fashion ranges need different price strategies. Products that are referred to as 'opening price point' (OPP) are high in volume and usually low in price. High-fashion items, which involve more risk than basic items, will command a higher price and therefore create a wider margin.

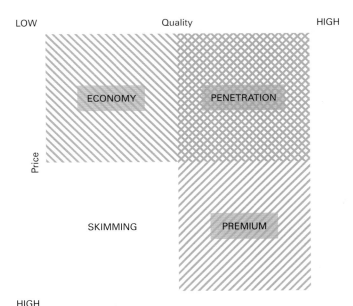

3.9 The Price Matrix Diagram

Fashion retailers use a price matrix to plan a pricing structure across different levels of products on offer. Penetration pricing involves setting prices artificially low to drum up interest in the product. Price skimming involves charging an unnecessarily high price to create a sense of exclusivity; this strategy is often used when launching a new or innovative product to the market.

An important part of the pricing strategy is to determine customers' spending patterns and average spend per range. It is usual for most fashion brands and retailers to use a price matrix within which they segment ranges into 'good, better and best'. This matrix can help fashion retailers to plan a pricing structure across different levels of fashion products on offer.

The marketing mix: people

A key element of a successful retail strategy is its people: those who understand the relevant technologies in the fashion industry and are able to perform the tasks necessary to meet the development objectives of the business. This goes hand in hand with business infrastructure in terms of organization, recruiting capabilities, employee benefit programmes, customer support facilities and its logistical capabilities.

Fashion retailing can be a difficult and volatile business; it requires making quick, risky decisions about fast-moving fashion items. In fashion retailing there are two key roles: the buyers and the merchandisers; these are the people who ensure that the fashion retailer has the right products in the right place at the right time.

The competence of the management team and the 'stars' within it can not be overlooked: it is important to manage talent within a business.

Also, part of people management within retail strategy is the retailer's ability to form successful designer collaborations. Topshop and H&M are well-known for their designer ranges – notable examples are Balmain and Karl Lagerfeld at H&M and Christopher Kane and Preen at Topshop.

3.10 Proenza Schouler
This model is wearing a Proenza Schouler tuxedo walking in the New York Fashion week runway show.

Retail experts

There are many internationally renowned business experts and retailers who understand the market and who know how to attract and keep the right talent in terms of design, buying, sourcing and merchandising.

Andrew Rosen is a great example of a retail expert and 'merchant' running large-scale, successful fashion organizations; after setting up and selling Theory, Rosen invested in emerging designers.

These include Alice + Olivia, Rag & Bone and Proenza Schouler. Rosen also has stakes in Kiki de Montparnasse, Aiko and Gryphon. Andrew Rosen was one of the first to identify the gap in the US and international markets for fashionable contemporary brands. Other 'big names' in global fashion retail include Millard 'Mickey' Drexler (former CEO of Gap and J.Crew) and Jose Neves of Farfetch. Many European high-street names have expanded internationally such as The Kooples, Sandro, Acme, Claudie Pierlot and Comptoir des Cotonniers.

3.11 Hudson Yards New York
Here we can see the newest shopping area in New York, the Hudson Yards, with 'the vessel' designed by Thomas Heatherwick. It houses a boutique collection of stores and products in the first shopping mall in Manhattan.

The role of the buyer

Along with the designer, the fashion buyer is crucial to the success of fashion retailing and range planning. Fashion buyers are expected to be one step ahead of the market, continually seeking out forthcoming trends, what they refer to as 'newness'. As retailers have focused increasingly upon designing and producing their own designs, the importance of the team involved in buying, merchandising, product design and development cannot be emphasized enough. Buyers need to take calculated risks at times with huge budgets but must also recognize the demands and needs of the core customers.

A fashion buyer for a high-street chain such as H&M will work with suppliers and in-house design teams to identify and develop the trends for the next season. Buyers for bigger stores will work with brands to buy selected items from a collection, or may work directly with suppliers to modify a trend that will best suit their target market for their own brands. The buyer must have a good eye for fashion with a keen business sense. A common misconception is that a buying role is design-led. While there are elements of creativity, the most important skill is to think commercially because, ultimately, the items must sell well.

Fashion buying as a career

A retail buyer is responsible for planning and selecting a range of products to sell in retail outlets, which may be physical stores, online or both. The buyer must consider several factors when making purchasing decisions including customer demand, price, quality and availability.

Market trends, store policy and financial budgets are other considerations and restraints. As a buyer you'll source new merchandise and review existing items to ensure products remain competitive. By fully understanding customer needs, you are able to maximize profits and provide a commercially viable range of merchandise at competitive prices. Keeping up to date with market trends and reacting to changes in demand are key elements of the role; working closely with design and product development is often a critical element. Retail buyers have a considerable amount of responsibility and autonomy in what is often a pressured environment.

Responsibilities of a buyer

Throughout the year, the responsibilities of a buyer may be numerous and changeable, due to the fast pace in which the fashion industry changes thanks to technology and trends continuously developing. However, their responsibilities may include:

× Analyzing consumer buying patterns and predicting future trends

× Regularly reviewing performance indicators, such as sales and discount levels

× Managing plans for stock levels

× Reacting to changes in demand and logistics

× Meeting suppliers and negotiating terms of contract

× Maintaining relationships with existing suppliers and sourcing new suppliers and designers for future products

× Understanding the basic rules of vendor management, allocation and price negotiation

3.12 Jigsaw
Models pose at the A by Jigsaw Presentation during London Fashion Week.

× Liaising with other departments within the organization to ensure projects are completed

× Attending trade fairs, in the UK and overseas, to select and assemble a new collection of products

× Participating in promotional activities

× Writing reports and forecasting sales levels

× Presenting new ranges to senior retail managers

× Liaising with shop personnel to ensure supply meets demand

× Getting feedback from customers

UK retailer Jigsaw closely coordinates its design activities with the merchandising and buying teams and remains in close contact with suppliers to ensure product quality and consistency are maintained throughout production. One quality that all good fashion buyers tend to share is tacit knowledge: the ability to instinctively know when something is right or on trend. This knowledge cannot easily be taught, although it may evolve over time: it cannot be described as anything other than flair and acumen for the product and a love of fashion itself. It is an exciting job role but not easy; at times it is highly pressurized, requiring great stamina and the ability to act quickly and with accuracy. Some buyers may have been trained in a non-fashion environment with a company that they may not initially have considered working for. Often the large international retailers will have the best training programmes, which are well worth considering.

Renowned buyers

Buyers with international reputations include Natalie Kingham at Matches, London. There are many others at large retailers whose skill set lies in editing collections for their customers and seeking out new and different brands and new fashion designers. These talented individuals can make designers famous and add considerable gravitas to their success. Joan Burstein, the founder and owner of Browns, London, helped launch the careers for many up-and-coming designers, including John Galliano, Christopher Kane, Mark Fast and Gareth Pugh. Browns is now owned by Farfetch and also has Browns East in Hackney, London and carries on this tradition by stocking many cutting edge brands.

Independent retailers are often those with risk-taking owners and buyers who want to support new labels.

Concept stores are a further retail extension of independents. They are often very influential on the fashion industry as a total lifestyle look from clothing to home to food.

Some of the most well known of these global names include:

× Corso Como (with stores in South Korea, New York and Shanghai)
× Dover Street Market
× The British House Beijing
× Browns East London
× Nous Paris
× Store X Berlin

3.13 Corso Como, Milan
Corso Como 10, the concept store, combining an art gallery, bookshop, hotel and restaurant into one, located in Milan, Italy.

The role of the merchandiser

The merchandiser is the analytical and numerate figure of the key product development trio of designer, buyer and merchandiser.

The fashion merchandiser is involved in forecasting stock levels and analyzing trends, allocating the stock and monitoring the sales of fashion products (and the colour and size in each style). Merchandisers will often talk about 'cover' of the stock levels, which refers to the number of weeks that stock is available for; there are many different ways of forecasting this cover and managing it in conjunction with suppliers. They will oversee deliveries and work very closely with manufacturers. These are the people who decide and agree big budgets, coordinate and assimilate clever promotions and maximize opportunities for the fashion ranges to be bought and developed.

Merchandisers and buyers work together to agree stock levels and allocation. This involves allocating different ranges per store and which of these are to be volume or trial products. They will leave some level of fluidity within the budget allowing for in-season decisions for top-up orders or cancellations and room for the latest trend-led items. This is often referred to as 'open to buy' (OTB).

Fashion merchandising as a career

Fashion merchandising is a key function of most fashion retailers who work very closely with the design, product development, buying and distribution teams.

Merchandisers ensure that products appear in the right store, or on a website, at the appropriate time and in the correct quantities. This involves working closely with the buying teams to accurately forecast trends, plan stock levels and monitor performance. While the buyer selects the lines, the merchandiser decides how much money should be spent, how many lines should be bought, and in what quantities.

In smaller companies, the same person may be responsible for both buying and merchandising.

Merchandisers play a key role within retail, as profits can be affected by how successfully they undertake their work. Merchandisers set prices to maximize profits and manage the performance of ranges, planning promotions and markdowns as necessary. They also oversee delivery and distribution of stock and deal with suppliers.

Responsibilities

Duties vary depending on the company and the particular retail sector, but will typically include planning of product ranges, preparing sales, and stock plans in conjunction with buyers. Other responsibilities might include

× Liaising with buyers, analysts, stores, suppliers and distributors

× Maintaining a comprehensive library of appropriate data

× Working closely with visual-display staff and department heads to decide how goods should be displayed to maximize sales

× Producing layout plans for stores, sometimes called 'statements'

× Forecasting profits and sales, and optimizing the sales volume and profitability of designated product areas

× Planning budgets and presenting sales forecasts and figures for new ranges

× Controlling stock levels based on forecasts for the season

× Using specialist computer software, for example to handle sales statistics, produce sales projections and present spreadsheets and graphs

× Analyzing every aspect of bestsellers (for example, the bestselling price points, colours or styles) and ensuring that they reach their full potential

× Maintaining awareness of competitors' performance

× Monitoring slow sellers and taking action to reduce prices or set promotions as necessary

× Gathering information on customers' reactions to products

× Analyzing the previous season's sales and reporting on the current season's lines

× Making financial presentations to senior managers

× Accompanying buyers on visits to manufacturers to appreciate production processes

× Meeting with suppliers and managing the distribution of stock, by negotiating cost prices, ordering stock, agreeing timescales and delivery dates and completing the necessary paperwork identifying production and supply difficulties and dealing with any problems or delays as they arise (source adapted from AGCAS Graduate Prospects Ltd, 2019)

To conclude, in the fashion retail environment buying and merchandising are crucial roles. The merchandisers are expected to bring the 'science' to match the 'art' brought by the buyer. However, in the digital age it is important to note these lines between the roles are blurred and although there are specific job descriptions different brands have their own ways of managing buying and merchandising and there is greater flexibility between the two roles to reflect the needs of the industry and retailer.

Interview

Richard Hurtley, Founder and Managing Director, Rich Insight

Richard Hurtley started his retail journey in just his second year of university. He created a brand, Rampant Sporting, starting with just four colour ways of socks and a website, which would become a multi-channel retailer with a small store portfolio, shows business, e-commerce platform and wholesale offering. As a result, Richard dealt with retailers including department stores John Lewis and House of Fraser to e-tailers like ASOS and Amazon.

Richard now runs Rich Insight, a consultancy focused on supporting many brands, not exclusively fashion, and focusses on getting into new markets and online.

How important is it for fashion retailers to have a clear strategy?

I think that in fashion just like any other business you need to know your purpose and understand the objectives with clarity and make decisions on how to achieve these. Fashion is such a complex industry with its inherent size, variance and seasonality plus having to back up what you do with delivery. However, this makes it both challenging and rewarding, you must be crystal clear about what makes your brand stand out and leverage the points of difference and effectiveness. You must have a clarity of vision and be able to future plan as it is so competitive – there are so many great products brands and designers out there and your strategy will give your purpose, otherwise there is too much risk.

How often do you feel that a retail strategy and overall retail formats and business models need to be reviewed?

If we are talking routes to market and sales channels these should be monitored daily and looking at performance and monthly in more detail to review what has gone well and what you can do to manipulate sales for the future. On product, a monthly reviews of lines is a minimum. Weekly trading meetings are important often this is the difference between being more tactical than strategic and overall yearly it is important to question things and evaluate where more change is required. Change in retail is accelerated around us and we need a process and place that can adapt and should avoid making broad assumptions. I would look to realistically to review strategy every six months and decide and ask questions such as 'how am I doing am I there?' and of course 'how can I improve?' And ask yourself 'is this channel still relevant?'. Sometimes we are all too busy running the ship so a full review every 6–12 months is more realistic.

The changes in fashion retail, in terms of speed to market, and the changes brought about by digital innovation have impacted on designers and brands. How do you view these?

It is very much a mix of good and bad news in terms of innovation – there are of course quicker routes online instead of what used to be the tried and tested models. Different Business Models are in place including B2B domestic agents, and representatives and wholesale still has a presence. Distributors and brands taking out licenses in new territories – slice of margin – fashion brands have often licensed for example in areas such as homeware. Overall I would say there are two major digital disruptors in retail:

1. Marketplace

The first one is absolutely key and is the marketplace model – it is the area that has changed in retail the most and most distributors have been squeezed because of this. Brands are going direct to customers. So many brands use this direct to consumer model and there are many 'pure play' start up websites in fashion – Finery is a good example of this. Wholesale sales are small – most online retail creates opportunities for example Shopify will set up a site for £38 per month and it is industry best practice. Online has been a leveller – websites are so much more affordable and brands can integrate their applications with these web platforms. Marketplaces are completely stealing the lunch from wholesalers and have to all extents cut out that channel – some examples here include Zalando, E-bay etc; these platforms go direct to consumer. Brands sell through these platforms to own customer information and sales data and this compliments e-commerce. Even in the domestic market – the skill set of a 3rd party platform that has an existing market already it is a basic best practice for many brands.

2. Innovation in Logistics

There are two major digital disruptors. The second is innovation in logistics which has created better deliveries, better or free returns which are very straightforward and customers are less likely to return product with a problem. The innovation in technology is being used to determine sizing and fit. Additionally, there are many returns lockers for consumers for example in the UK we have facilities such as Doddle and there is so much in the logistical infrastructure with other drop-off locations and brands are also utilizing other programmes and retailers to deliver or return goods. It is certainly a challenge to stand out in the noise. Retailers need to try to attract more online traffic and tap into new markets internationally.

How has online and digital affected the key ways in which fashion retailers operate?

The brought in digital support on the core value proposition (going back to the area of retail strategy) has made a difference to the competition and in fact having a focused business can work in your favour. Strong product will always have routes to market – the digital – video storytelling with rich content online including lifestyle content is important to make fashion product stand out, though also the operational side is important in terms of service and logistical technology across the board.

Fashion start-ups have the ability to set up cheaply and quickly without legacy challenges – enabled by technology and innovation digital sales can happen without huge investment. Small brands are pioneering retail recharged – they can utilize great amounts of efficiencies for minimal cost software. High budgets for technology are not essential for emerging brands – existing ones have to move away from legacy existing systems.

The high-street environment and its purpose as a showroom and experience has three key issues including a large inventory online, growth in e-commerce (big change in competition), and emerging social media.

The high street has been hit by a predominance of Amazon which had 7.9 percent in 2018 of all fashion sold in USA and Walmart had 8.6 percent of all fashion sold by comparison. This is a major change – fashion is one of the biggest markets in world and it's a huge change over a decade and is done largely direct to consumer.

What are the key changes in brands' sourcing and manufacturing linked to this?

First of all, there are large amounts of manufacturers wanting to go direct to consumers as private label creates a better margin for everyone – also Chinese suppliers selling on Amazon directly to customers is an increasing theme. Obviously, with online counterfeiting can be an issue but it's so easy to sell into new markets

Amazon and ebay cannot see everything that they are selling, but from a brand perspective there are more sites for sourcing opportunities – if you like it's a 'supply compass' creating access to 'en masse' suppliers and marketplaces for manufacturers platforms too such as Alibaba. Equally, there are online crowdsourced opinions and experiences with recommendations – even Linkedin is used by manufacturers to approach potential customers.

How you see the future of fashion retail strategy?

I think it has got a bright future in spite of a challenging time in the UK and the USA but it is difficult to convince investors into fashion. Any fashion brand can build change and adaptation into the business model the innovation is catalyzing and accelerating.

Retailers need to be able to adapt – and this should be woven in through digital all the way through from strategy to routes to market in an overarching way otherwise they are continually trying to keep up and have to be one step ahead. Brands will need to go back to roots of why they exist such as – good product knowledge and having a 'hero' item – its the new innovation is what sets them apart.

The homogenized retail format of 'every street corner' approach will just not work anymore, the experience is key, and weirdly the high street can in fact be the most interesting. Amazon has been the cause of many retailers demise but it forced people to blame them for a lot of this disruption and whatever the reason Amazon have been a catalyst – online. Amazon are going to take over physical stores and be online. Retail can just be a commodity and brands need to become either convenience or experience.

For example in Seattle – for convenience you can use a phone to buy a sandwich on Amazon – so they are already there – moving into high street. They will continue to take strategically placed real estate but are analytically driven and are planning 800 stores in USA. This will probably happen elsewhere such as the UK market.

Brands who are agile and can take a profitable multi-channel approach in an area where others struggle, (many fashion retailers compete with each other rather than trying to collaborate) can win. Short term decision making is not good strategy – successful long term businesses have a well thought-out business model and will succeed with a mixture of tactics and strategy.

Case Study
Farfetch

Many retail 'platforms' now exist for fashion brands to sell their fashion products. However, some are considered more innovative and influential on the industry as a whole. One of the most innovative retail models around is Farfetch, founded by José Neves in 2007.

The company focusses on luxury products and has rapidly expanded internationally since its inception. It now includes media and industry support such as the conference and support for start-up brands. Following is a timeline of the key activities starting with October 2008 when Farfetch launched, initially selling products from twenty-five boutiques in five countries.

Product

The supply of products comes from sixty-four boutiques. The first Farfetch offices opened in the USA (Los Angeles) and in Brazil (Sao Paolo). The partnership network includes over 300 boutiques in thirty-five countries. More boutiques were added more recently in new markets and in addition to first direct brand partners who joined the platform, such as Japan and Australia. Local offices are in Asia including China and Hong Kong. Farfetch now has almost 500 boutique partners and 200 direct brand partners.

Store of the future

In May 2015 Farfetch acquired the iconic British boutique Browns and launched a new concept Store of The Future. This innovative business unit includes Farfetch Black & White which is Farfetch's flagship, an e-commerce white-label for luxury fashion brands. The company also has launched its Dream Assembly technology accelerator and acquired Curiosity in July to expand its social media efforts in China. Fashion Concierge is another recent acquisition.

There are links between these initiatives and most competitors have launched data and analytics, supported by the ecosystem of the host brand. The supply chain is a common area of focus for retail innovation, as are payments. Many of the brands involved have strengthened their offer through the control and in-house capability of a private-label range and launched digital content platforms to generate revenue. All of these point to Farfetch as the platform of choice in an increasingly competitive luxury segment.

International expansion

JD.com and Farfetch partnered to open the ultimate gateway for bringing luxury brands to China. In February 2018 Farfetch partnered with the Chalhoub Group to build a leading platform for luxury in the Middle East. Chanel and Farfetch have an exclusive partnership involving customized retail experiences in Chanel boutiques. Also, Farfetch has partnered with its first department store partner, Harvey Nichols in London.

3.14 Farfetch
Here we see the founder of Farfetch, Jose Neves, Business of Fashion Imran Amed, and Marco Bizzarri speaking at The Business of Fashion presents VOICES in the UK.

This reflects the important mixture of online and offline and a trend for 'pureplayers' to extend their reach into physical stores to compete further and disrupt the market.

The Dream Assembly model
Farfetch has a technology accelerator called 'Dream Assembly', a mentorship programme for start-ups worldwide. This support for start-up brands creates networking opportunities and highlights the importance of passing on knowledge to create a new generation of blended fashion and technology experts.

Farfetch believes that the whole luxury fashion industry can benefit from helping to support the next generation with the

ambition to shape the future of commerce. The Dream Assembly programme is run from Lisbon and includes workshops, sessions with senior leaders at Farfetch plus mentorship meetings covering topics such as e-commerce, marketing, technology, supply chain and logistics and provides start-up brands with access to the expertise of Farfetch. The Dream Assembly also facilitates networking and devised a workshop with Burberry for its members.

Farfetch OS conference
Farfetch hosted a conference for brands, called Farfetch OS and unveiled a version of Store of The Future technology and simultaneously a 90-minute delivery service in ten cities across four continents. They

also have partnered with the publishing giant Conde Nast to create global content.

Farfetch launched a conference – FarfetchOS – to drive change and promote innovation as part of the future of luxury fashion.

The conference took place at the Design Museum in London as founder José Neves joined with Natalie Massenet about the future of luxury. There was also a tour of Farfetch's Store of the Future.

Farfetch tailors its technology for each partner city and store. The Store of the Future at the Design Museum showed the way that technology can be used as part of the customer journey and is available in the Browns Store in London.

Digital service

Farfetch offers customers an opportunity to 'opt-in' to data sharing as part of their shopping experience. When a customer arrives in the store and uses a log in, the sales team receives a notification that a customer has arrived. Then they can glean an insight in recent shopping behaviour provided on the customers profile. It tells them which brands that customer has looked at and purchased.

> '[Farfetch] was born out of a deep love of fashion and a profound belief that fashion is an essential expression of individuality and what makes each of us unique.'
>
> – José Neves

Radio frequency ID tags (RFID) and shopping

Using RFID technology and ultrasound in the connected clothing rail, Farfetch is able to recognize any product that customers pick up and can then create a wish list and product selection. The sales teams can see their in-store wish list and use it to recommend products.

The Store of the Future team developed software to enhance different versions of a changing room. Farfetch took digital displays and mirrors and developed software connected to the Farfetch platform. These included a connected mirror showing the customer's digital wish list. The clients could then purchase items directly through the mirror.

Neves advises: 'Physical retail accounts for 93% of sales today, and even with online growing at fast speed, it will account for 80% by 2025. Retailers need a way to collect information about their customers while they are browsing in-store, just as they collect data from online searches. Store of the Future aims at providing the in-store experience of the future by giving visibility to retailers on what is happening in the store. It's the offline cookie that closes the loop, between a great online presence and a complete omni-channel offering and, finally in-store technology which augments the experience of customers in store and overall. The next stage in the evolution of the fashion industry is the connected store, which uses technology to enhance the luxury retail experience to become even more customer centric. Farfetch is at the crossroads of luxury and technology and is well placed to understand its needs and deliver a tailored solution' (Neves, 2018).

Chapter summary

This chapter has examined the concept of retail strategy and the ways in which a fashion business addresses the increasingly competitive marketplace. We have seen that it is important to identify and analyze the competition and to understand the business's strengths and weaknesses alongside those of the competition. In addition, we discussed the components for strategic analysis: market position, place, price and people. A regular review of the strength and viability of fashion products and the provision of customer service is essential for a successful retail strategy.

Questions and discussion points

We have examined the ways in which fashion businesses develop retail strategy; consider the following questions in connection with this and your understanding of Chapter 3:

1. Identify the different types of fashion retailers in your local shopping area. What are the key differences that you see between the retail formats?

2. Identify some retailers' own brands or labels and analyze them: how similar are they compared with the well-known brands available?

3. How effective are fashion multi-brand platforms at presenting new designers' ranges and introducing new innovative product offers? Consider independents and any concept stores.

4. What sort of promotions or sales do you see at the moment? How effective are they?

5. How do these sales or promotions differ by retailer? What sort of price ranges can you identify and what are the levels of discount?

Exercises

The following exercises are designed to make you think like a buyer or merchandiser. They are known in the fashion industry as comparative shop exercises and are regularly conducted as part of competitive analysis.

1. Visit two different retailers in two different types of market sector. Analyze the competition to these retailers: who are they competing with and why?

2. Visit the websites of retailers that are 'pure players' online and those that are multi-channel retailers. What differences, if any, do you see?

3. Price: what are the key differences of products that you see online and in stores in different price categories? Are there differences in relation to fabric, design, colour, packaging or designer labels?

4. In your opinion, and based on your research, put a list together of the top ten products you have found based on good price, quality and fashionability.

5. Try to develop a new strategy for a company or brand that you consider to be 'tired' or in need of a makeover. What would you like to do differently?

The Fashion Supply Chain

In this chapter we examine supply chain management (SCM) and consider why it is important to the fashion business. If fashion retailers and businesses get it right, SCM has massive potential rewards. There is a fast-growing belief amongst fashion retailers that all people involved in the supply chain – from designers, buyers and merchandisers to suppliers and production managers – should have in-depth working knowledge of all the functions. It is vital to understand that SCM begins with the customer and that it does not end with them. Successful fashion supply chains compete for business as much as individual fashion brands do. Logistics and efficiency blended with technology can deliver the vision of designers to customers. Sustainability is now not a 'nice to have' element but should be embedded in all successful fashion supply chain strategy.

4.1 Sri Lanka Colombo
Sri Lanka houses world-class manufacturing of fashion clothing for many global brands and has innovated machinery, including recycling water in several factory units.

Background of the textile industry and supply chains

The fashion business is one of the most global and internationalized business types from retail to manufacturing and raw materials.

It is useful to understand industrialization, within the context of the textiles industry, in order to examine supply chain management in more detail. It is also important to consider the fact that fashion is the second most polluting industry globally after the oil industry and this is very obvious in the supply chain due to these key fashion factors:

× Volatility

× Short shelf life

× Huge variety

× Hard to standardize

Manufacturing of textiles is high investment in machinery but low in labour; manufacturing of finished clothing is low investment in machinery, high investment in labour.

Let us consider the history and context of fashion and supply chains and according to Bell (1963), the industrialization of countries can be divided into three categories:

× Pre-industrial

× Industrial

× Post-industrial

A key characteristic of a post-industrial society is a growth in the service sector of activity and employment. This includes fashion retailing, which is a significant part of the service sector.

4.2 Textile Factory Workers
We see here a historical image of workers in the John Smedley Factory in Matlock, UK.

The UK, the USA and Canada, Australia, Japan and most countries in the EU have evolved from being industrial to post-industrial economies. Pre-industrial economies include countries where there are still large cottage industries: most of Africa, for example, and the Indian sub-continent. China is a notable example of a country that has moved to the industrial phase.

Textiles were a major part of the 'first' industrial revolution, centred in Lancashire in the UK. Manchester, in the UK, was known as the 'Cottonopolis'; it has been described as the first global industrial city. The industrial revolution of the textile industry rapidly spread to northern Europe in the late eighteenth century and then to the USA. We have witnessed a new industrial revolution in China and SE Asia, developed in a much shorter period of time.

Multi-Fibre Arrangement

The Multi-Fibre Arrangement (MFA) was established in 1974 to govern world trade in textiles and garments. Under the MFA, Canada, the USA and the EU imposed quotas on the amount of apparel and textiles that could be imported from seventy-three developing countries, mostly in Asia. The quotas were phased out over a ten-year period and finally eliminated on 1 January 2005. This opened China up to unlimited volumes of supply and its world class manufacturing but has arguably contributed to the increase in huge volumes of 'fast fashion' across the globe.

Latterly, the rise of technology and robotics is creating what is often referred to as the fourth Industrial Revolution, which has the potential to further transform fashion supply chains.

However, in the fashion business the wants and needs of the customer remain always top priority. Manufacturing fashion in diverse locations from Europe to China, Sri Lanka and India has historically created opportunities to see first hand the wealth of textiles and techniques available across the globe.

What is fast fashion?

There are several key concepts in SCM that have emerged over the last twenty years. These include so-called fast fashion or quick response models. Collaborative relationships in SCM, where relevant in the chain, are crucial to global supply chain success. Ethical issues have emerged as a result of international sourcing, creating a real need for these relationships to be based upon trust and shared values of the supplier and brand.

Next we consider the 4Rs of the supply chain:

The 4Rs

Martin Christopher developed the theory known as the 4Rs, which works in a similar way to the marketing mix. It is tactical and should be applied to each supply chain: reliability; resilience; responsiveness and relationships. These key factors should be considered by brands and retailers when developing or changing and managing the supply chain strategy.

'"Fast fashion" is a term used to describe a new accelerated fashion business model that has evolved since the 1980s. It involves increased numbers of new fashion collections every year, quick turnarounds and often lower prices. Reacting rapidly to other new products to meet consumer demand is crucial to this business model.'
— UK Gov Report, 2018

Lean and agile

Naylor et al (1999) provide a useful definition of the two paradigms as follows:

'Agility means using market knowledge and a virtual corporation to exploit profitable opportunities in a volatile marketplace. . . . Leanness means developing a value stream to eliminate all waste including time, and to enable a level schedule.'

Lean and agile

Fast fashion models of supply or quick response (QR) manufacturing techniques accelerated the impact for more effective supply chain management in the last decade. QR is defined as 'a search for a reduction in lead times' (Christopher, 2000) and helped to establish relationships in supply chains.

Although fashion retailer Zara is credited with introducing fast fashion to the mass market, it did in fact grow out of QR techniques developed some years before. Described as the evolution of lean and agile supply chains, QR manufacturing developed in the USA, with retailers and manufacturers who had to respond to a loss in market share to suppliers from the Far East in the 1980s. Quick response (QR) is a market-driven business strategy focused on providing shorter lead times. QR enables orders to be placed closer to the start of the selling season and, typically for fashion products, QR lowers lead time by one to four months (Skinner, 1992).

Fashion SCM strategy

The SCM strategy of a fashion business should reflect the company and its business strategy. An effective supply chain strategy should be market-driven and customer focused, with strong links between the buying and product development processes. Good critical path management is absolutely crucial to the success of SCM strategy; it closely monitors the progress of each step from product development to production.

SCM strategy is driven by globalization and fast-fashion retail models. Businesses should focus on their core competencies – in other words, they must consider what they are good at.

USP

Prahalad and Hamel (1994) define USP as 'a bundle of skills and technology that enables a business to provide a benefit to customers.'

Some of the key points for a fashion business supply chain to review include:

× Cost
× Speed to market
× Reliability
× Flexibility
× Responsiveness (ability to react to sales)

These points can all contribute to making a business/retailer unique or special, often referred to as the unique selling point (USP).

Relationships in SCM

Relationships in SCM are vital to success: buyers, merchandisers and designers alike need to understand the implications of supply chain decisions and decide together where it is appropriate to add value and where they need to reduce cost. An effective supply chain creates value for the customer at an acceptable cost, margin and selling price.

There are many types of suppliers and manufacturers available to fashion retailers and they can provide different levels of service.

Supplier types

It is important to consider what is required and to build good relationships in supply chains where they are most needed. There are three main supplier types:

1. **Direct supply**
    The retailer has total control of the process, which requires a high level of input; this is often referred to as 'buying FOB' (the ex-factory price = freight on board). The retailer arranges own transport and duty and sends all the information to the manufacturer. This is by far the most common method in the mass market and provides more control and often better margin for the retailer brand.

2. **Agent**
    This is a sales and design team that acts as a go-between, arranging visits, managing orders, fielding calls and negotiations. Agents such as Li and Fung, based in Hong Kong, are known as global 'super sourcers' and they work with hundreds of factories and retailers in south-east Asia.

3. **Full-service vendor (FSV)**
    This is usually a world-class, large-scale manufacturer, which can offer benefits for retailers. The FSV will organize transportation, duty and all exportation, providing good service levels from first samples to final-fit approval.

When making decisions about which suppliers to work with, the following must be considered: lead times, communication and costs involved to the retailer as well as reliability, ability and flexibility. Different products require different types of supplier; it is not a case of 'one size fits all'. The brand position in the market may also dictate the level of control and involvement the brand wishes to exercise.

Verticality in supply chains

The Japanese were at the forefront of innovation in supply chain relationships in the automobile industry and were one of the first to invest in the chain of manufacturing. This led to semi-vertical relationships via collaboration and coordination in the chain as well as investment in people. This type of collaboration then spread to the clothing industry with techniques such as 'just in time' (JIT): 'a common supply chain concept in the apparel industry; it is the delivery of finished goods without carrying excess stock but in time to meet the market demand' (Bruce, 2004). Vertical supply chains are really restricted to those with the most money, luxury brands being largely semi-vertical or vertical in their approach.

Supply chain trends and drivers for change

There are a number of current drivers and trends of SCM and global sourcing trends. These range from firstly the combination of reduced labour costs and a readily available, flexible workforce that enables shorter critical path or lead times – essential for fast fashion. The second is advances in technology: the increased speed of the Internet and the evolution of trend forecasting websites have provided fashion retailers with fast access to catwalk trends. Technological changes, such as artificial intelligence, robotics in manufacturing, and digitalization of processes including 3D printing, have made replication of products easier and faster.

Technology in fashion supply chains

The fashion industry, like many others, has been impacted by the Fourth Industrial revolution and the advent of digitization. Supply Chain 4.0 embraces key areas where technology can assist us with the important areas of transparency and sustainability through its application including logistics and manufacturing. The Blockchain technology process, where every step from raw materials to finished goods is recorded and is immutable, has been introduced to further support transparency and accountability.

These areas include:

× RFID

× Blockchain

× Artificial intelligence

× Digital printing

× Use of robotics

Finally, and most importantly, sustainability and alternative consumption methods are increasingly significant. Recycled raw materials using ocean waste plastic or turning 'old' fabrics into new are being addressed in fashion supply chains as a way forward.

4.3 RFID Technology, Hong Kong
Former investment banker turned scientist, Yan Wa-tat, holds pearls containing radio-frequency
identification (RFID) chips and small cases with RFID chips inside.

'The goal of a digital supply chain is to fully integrate
and make visible every aspect of the movement of goods.
The key to this critical element of Industry 4.0 is big data
analytics. Already, companies have the tools to describe
much of the current state of their supply chains — where the
goods are, where the demand for specific items is currently
coming from, and when items are likely to be delivered. And
companies are learning to predict critical elements of the
chain. Demand through the chain can be better anticipated
thanks to more sophisticated signals from the market, which
translates to demand for production capacity, storage and
logistics needs, and changes in raw materials requirements.'
– PWC The State of Fashion, 2018

Global sourcing and world class supply chain models

Supply chain management in the fashion business has represented a paradigm shift in the manufacturing of goods. What this has meant in recent times is a shift from local to global sourcing. Globalization has had both positive and negative effects on manufacturing and purchasing behaviour alike. There is a trend towards balancing this out and we have seen attempts to move to a more 'local' or 'glocal' sourcing policy by many fashion brands – that is to say a more balanced strategy in supply chain management driven partly by sustainability and cost.

There is a framework which can be applied to supply chains that can be used to illustrate world class manufacturing and superior supply chain performance, known as the 'Triple-A Supply Chain' (Lee, 2004). Triple-A supply chains are those that exhibit agility, adaptability, and alignment. For instance, the most successful companies work within supply chains that rapidly respond to short-term changes in immediate and ultimate customer demands (agility), adjust to long-term changes in economies and markets by restructuring the supply chain (adaptability), and integrate and coordinate business processes that result in an equitable sharing of risks, costs, and benefits with all participating partners (alignment).

1. Agility

Successful companies foster agility by:

× A change in thinking by designers and product developers by buying fabric and 'designing' into often 'greige' fabric

× Creation of shorter lead times on 'hot' items by using available fabric to provide the next new product

× Luxury brands foster agility through durability and craftsmanship and quality of raw materials as a point of difference

2. Adaptiveness

Successful companies foster adaptability by:

× Monitoring world economies to identify new supply bases and markets

× Using intermediaries to develop fresh suppliers and logistics infrastructure

× Evaluating the needs of the ultimate customer as well as immediate customers

× Creating flexible product designs

× Determining where products stand in terms of tech and product life cycles (Lee 2004)

3. Alignment

Successful companies foster alignment by:

× Freely exchanging information with suppliers and customers

× Clearly laying out roles and responsibilities for suppliers and customers

× Equitably sharing risks costs and gains of improvement

(Lee and Billington, 1995; Lee: 2004)

4.4 A Dress Made by 3D Printing
As seen in Las Vegas, a model presents the Chromat Adrenaline Dress made of 3D-printed panels and featuring Intel's Curie Module.

See Now Buy Now fashion collections in thes chain

SNBN promises consumers from the luxury end of the market that they can have the clothing they see on catwalks almost immediately with no need to wait, which has the potential to change the supply chain and fashion system and create opportunities for brands. However, it may also force all brands to become retailers with all of the associated risks of forecasting sales and complicates further the delicate balance of supply chains and enforces the view that digital is transforming the fashion landscape. There are several key enablers of SNBN in the supply chain, according to Greg Petro at First Insight retail intelligence, which include,

The use of artificial intelligence (AI)

– With the advent of AI and machine learning, retailers are now implementing new AI-based solutions such as 'Optimized Line Planning' (OLP). OLP pulls data from multiple sources – including historical sales data, trend data, competitive data, CRM data, social media feeds and forward-looking voice of consumer data – to create a single view of the customer types or 'personas'. These personas bring insight into which groups of product attributes will resonate best with each segment and offer the starting point of a line plan for the designers and merchants. This capability enables companies to mitigate the risk of committing to raw materials in advance, and reduce their time to market by shortening development and decision cycles. It allows designers and merchants to be more confident that their range plan will achieve their financial objectives.

Collaborating to connect with the customer in product creation and launch

– Many retailers understand that the voice of the customer needs to be at the heart of product creation, and are utilizing technology to gather input on style from the very beginning of the process. The data is then offered to designers, merchants, suppliers and everyone in between so they can share ideas, collaborate and streamline delivery of the right products at the right price – faster.

3D printing – While still in its early phases, 3D printing promises retailers the ability to plan and change their styles in the moment. The fashion industry suffers from overproduction, and 3D tech brings disruptive innovations to the very early stages of a product's life cycle, which can cut production, inventory, shipping and waste. It also invites shoppers into the creative process through co-designing rather than browsing racks. Adidas is currently experimenting with 3D knitting on-demand in stores, hinting at the greater role it might play in fashion production and retail in the years ahead.

Smaller deliveries – Some retailers are moving away from large deliveries to be more targeted, increase demand and generate buzz. This approach is often referred to as the 'scarcity effect' or 'when it's gone it's gone' (WIGIG).

Making it locally – More corporations are finding it makes sense to keep production onshore. While it's more expensive, long lead times for manufacturing overseas mean producing locally can be more profitable in the end. Domestic production enables greater control and flexibility and allows designers to make changes that would be more expensive than with overseas suppliers.

(Brun, A., Castelli.C. etal 2018)

4.5 Local Manufacturing
The production line of the French brand, 'Le Coq Sportif', showing garments being made locally in one of their factories in France.

Geographical areas of expertise examples

China

This region was originally famous for silk and cashmere, its tailoring skills and hand-embellished products. The ending of the MFA (see page 95) opened up this market and therefore its enormous and skilled labour force. China is the world's fastest-growing world economy and the government has made major investments in its technology, road and rail infrastructure. China is often referred to as the 'factory of the world'. It is currently investing in 'One Belt One Road' rail and sea links across Asia and Europe which has its origins in the original 'Silk Route'.

India

India is behind China in terms of volume, but has similar production capability and is investing in infrastructure and technology to bolster its position, with large-scale textile production, especially cotton and silk fibres. It specializes in colour; woven, printed cloth and denim. There is a widely available labour force that largely speaks and understands English. The Indian government has invested in its manufacturing industry to enable development and a rising young population has helped this.

Sri Lanka

Sri Lanka is an established world class manufacturer of fashion clothing, via joint ventures and also wholly owned

Sri Lankan companies. It has a well-established joint apparel association forum, with businesses intending to advance from manufacturing to becoming full service vendors.

Bangladesh

Together with 'newer regions' such as Cambodia and Vietnam – often referred to as China+1 for its satellite Chinese factories taking advantage of lower labour costs – Bangladesh has risen as a low-cost, high-volume region for fast fashion.

Turkey

Turkey's close proximity to Europe and wide availability of cotton jersey fabrics and denim makes it a good local manufacturing option for European brands. Transport links are well established and there is a solid understanding of the fashion industry with relatively sophisticated manufacturing. Well known for products such as nightwear and swimwear, it is often referred to as a fast fashion hub.

Mexico and Central America

Manufacturers here are vulnerable to cheaper overseas imports and are more expensive than those in Asia but are useful and relevant to USA brands and retailers who may have preferential duty and import rates (research 'Clothesource' online to find out more).

Italy

Italy is renowned as a centre of excellence and craftsmanship particularly in textiles, silk and leather. Traditionally centred in and around Prato and Como in northern Italy, the industry has declined and only the very exclusive brands can afford to manufacture here. The Italian government has protected the remaining industry to support the designers. However, in order to survive, many Italian companies employed migrant workers or else relocated overseas.

UK

The majority of UK manufacturing now comprises small and niche manufacturers, which tend to be specialist and expensive. Some examples include knitwear in Hawick, Scotland and John Smedley, which still produces its specialist knitwear in Derbyshire, England. Details of other UK manufacturers can be found from the UK Fashion and Textile Association; search online for 'UKFT' to find out more. There has over the last five years been a concerted effort to 'Make it British' and even high-street brands are balancing their overseas production with local products. Search online for 'Make It British' to find out more.

USA

As with Italy and the UK, garment manufacturing has declined, due to technological advances and imports of apparel and textiles. Manufacturing has become highly automated and must be labour-efficient to compete effectively with foreign manufacturers. Nearly half of garment manufacture is based in three states: California, North Carolina and Georgia. However once again there have been recent attempts to promote 'Made in the USA' and trade with big competitors such as China may be limited by the government to protect its remaining industry.

Sourcing in fashion is a moving target and nowhere is perfect; therefore having a balanced sourcing policy, whilst taking speed, cost, quality and minimizing damage to the environment and workers into account, should be the ultimate goal for brands and designers.

The effects of globalization in fashion supply chains

Cheap imports and greater efficiency opened up new markets, creating high demand and new opportunities. There has also been a shift in production to higher-value consumer goods such as cashmere and leather. Affordable 'luxury' has led to the democratization of the fashion industry and so-called 'masstige'.

This 'masstige' has also created employment growth in some parts of the world where manufacturing has become

centralized. Production and manufacturing has been relocated to low-cost countries with cheap, flexible labour. There are now more working women and there is a greater need for increased flexibility in the workplace.

However, the changing employment structure within post-industrialized countries has led to broad-scale polarization of income distribution, such as unemployment coupled with an ageing population. In the EU and USA there has been an increase of one-person households.

All of these issues create opportunities and threats for fashion retailers and there has been a change in the broad-scale structure of customer consumption.

4.6 Veja Shoes
Pauline Darris, founder of the Darris brand, is wearing Veja shoes with Darris flowers in Paris France. Veja uses recycled materials in its manufacturing and has a transparent supply chain process.

4.7 and 4.8 Sri Lankan Garment Factory
In Sri Lanka several exporters have collaborated and created a 'green factory'. Here we see Sri Lankan garment workers manufacture items for British retailer Marks and Spencers at a factory in Seeduwa, some 30 km north of Colombo.

The key to success is for retailers and designers to try to recognize and anticipate consumer change. Key differences and change in customer attitudes are crucial to retailers when devising product ranges and retail store formats and in redeveloping supply chains. It is only certain that change will occur even more rapidly in the future as globalization continues; its impact is felt most acutely in supply chains.

Michael Kobori, vice president of social and environmental sustainability at Levi Strauss & Co., explains that 'The company recently expanded its Partnership for Cleaner Textiles (PaCT) programme to four countries in Asia, which has so far delivered 20% savings in water and energy consumption for six key vendors. Next on the agenda is a new target to reach 40% savings by 2025'.

Sustainability in fashion supply chains

Fashion supply chains are predominantly driven by fast clothing and disposability; they rely on the ability of manufacturers to switch production on and off and the ability of the brand to relocate for speed to market and margin pressures. However, public pressure from campaigners and NGOs (non-government organizations) has created a major force for change. Retailers are being forced to pay closer attention to the way in which their goods are produced: bad publicity surrounding ethics is not good for business.

Fashion retailers and manufacturers must consider their global impact as they continue to develop products overseas and expand in new markets (both in terms of selling and manufacturing). The ethics of local and global supply, associated labour issues and their impact upon local communities are increasingly important.

Corporate social responsibility CSR and business ethics are often used interchangeably but are quite different. CSR is related to the social contract between a business and the society in which it operates. It sets out the intentions of the business to behave and operate responsibly with its sourcing and supply chain and in its overall business strategy. Most of the large-scale fashion businesses, such as Zara, H&M Uniqlo and many others including sportswear brands such as Nike and the luxury Kering Group of brands have a CSR policy embedded within their overall corporate and marketing strategy and this is widely promoted. CSR policy can usually be found on a company's website, illustrating how that brand or retailer implements this process. Businesses should apply CSR as part of their key performance measures and this can impact on the bottom line: profit. Cause-related marketing (CRM)

Ethical issues

× Fair trade
× Child labour
× Workers' rights and pay
× Working conditions
× Carbon footprint
× Organic textiles
× Air miles of clothing
× Animal welfare
× Textile technology: recycled and biodegradable fibres
× Global warming
× Supplier relationships

4.9 Recycled Fabrics New York
Fabscrap Operations Coordinator Sabina Montinar is holding some of the recycled fabrics at the company's warehouse in New York. The fashion industry generates tons of textile waste. Fabscrap provides pickup of fabric scraps from commercial businesses in New York, including fashion brands, interior designers and cutting rooms.

is an offshoot of CSR. The idea is that aligning companies with certain causes will create social capital in the business. Many fashion retailers use ethical initiatives and turn them into valuable marketing and corporate strategy, which may then be used to gain competitive advantage. It is clear that some fashion brands do far more than others to enhance the visibility and ethical nature of their supply chains. However, whilst responsible retailers may take an ethical stance in their marketing campaigns, this, alongside a demand for fast fashion, can present challenges; the two do not sit comfortably together.

The role of NGOs

NGOs are defined by the World Bank (1995) as 'private organizations that pursue activities to relieve suffering, promote the interests of the poor, protect the environment, provide basic social services, or undertake community development.'

Labour issues in the garment industry are well documented and it is the role of the NGOs to work with fashion retailers to establish and improve their labour policies and to help protect workers' rights. Examples include the International Labour Organization (ILO), a UN agency

4.10 Bangladeshi Textile Workers
Bangladeshi female workers work at a garment factory in Gazipur, outskirts of Dhaka. The garment sector of Bangladesh has provided employment opportunities to women from the rural areas that previously did not have any opportunity to be part of the formal workforce. Bangladesh is the world's second-largest apparel exporter of western (fast) fashion brands. Sixty percent of the export contracts of western brands are with European buyers and about forty percent with American buyers.

established in 1919, which is jointly governed by government, employer and worker representatives. Its mission is to raise global awareness and understanding of labour issues, to eliminate forced and child labour.

Labour Behind the Label in the UK is a network of organizations that support workers worldwide, helping them to 'improve their working conditions, through awareness raising, information provision and encouraging international solidarity between workers and consumers.' In addition to working in the industry, Labour Behind the Label works with colleges and

fashion students to promote knowledge and understanding of the issues that may confront buyers, merchandisers, designers and anyone else involved in sourcing.

The Common Objective (CO) is another such organization which promotes collaboration through Sustainability:

'According to the UN there are nearly 1.3 million factories and mills involved in garment supply chains. Approximately half produce garments and the rest other stages of the supply chain including spinning and fabric mills. China dominates

More than half the world's supply of fibres and fabrics comes from Asia, with China producing more than a quarter. Global textile mills are worth $667.5 billion, similar in size to the Swiss economy and that value is set to grow by more than 26%, while fibre production could rise by up to 5% per year to 2025. . .' (CO, 2018).

The ETI

Fashion retailers' policies vary wildly but should all be based on the guidelines set out by the World Trade Organization (WTO). A member organization called the Ethical Trading Initiative (ETI) is a good example of an NGO that is influencing and helping shape retail policy. The initiative, launched in the UK in 1997, bases its policies on WTO guidelines. It is relevant to note here that there is little, if any, legislation in place to force retailers and manufacturers to join an organization such as the ETI and to adhere to guidelines. But by becoming a member, a company is making a commitment to tackle issues within its supply chains. The ETI's member companies are expected to report annually on their efforts and results and to show improvement in their ethical trade performance.

ETI Company members include ASOS, Asda, Gap, Inditex Group (which owns Zara), Levi Strauss, Next, Reiss, New Look, Boden, Primark and Tesco.

Some fashion brands do far more than others in order to make the necessary changes and improve conditions for workers. Sourcing policy varies between different retailers and brands and although there are similar codes of practice to those of the ETI they are open to interpretation. It is essential that

Below is the ETI base code from the Ethical Trade Initiative, designed on WTO guidelines:

× Employment is freely chosen
× Freedom of association and the right to collective bargaining are respected
× Working conditions are safe and hygienic
× Child labour shall not be used
× Living wages are paid
× Working hours are not excessive
× No discrimination is practised
× Regular employment is provided
× No harsh or inhumane treatment is allowed

(Ethical Trading Initiative, 2018)

Search online for 'WTO' and 'ETI' base code, to find out more from their websites.

brands and retailers work closely with suppliers, giving them time and help in order to achieve the required standards. Monitoring suppliers, minimizing risk and solving short-term problems together can make fashion businesses more efficient as well as ethical. It may mean a rise in costs but should also mean an increase in sales and profit margins.

Kering Group strategy on sustainability

Marie Claire Daveu, Kering Group Director of Sustainability, believes that 'We live in a time when sustainability is no longer an option and our future depends on it. We have no other choice as business it must change the old system that does not benefit our planet and our need to be part of the solution. Fashion is at a cross roads

4.11 Cotton Harvest, Turkey
A view of a cotton field during harvesting season in Cukurova district of Adana, Turkey.

and decisions made now will have far reaching consequences. So, our industry footprint will only increase if we do not make changes.'

There are many ways we can implement recycling and reuse into fashion supply chains, including recovering and reselling items customers no longer want, and hiring or renting clothing and developing 'subscription' models, which enable customers to swap clothes but also incentivize retailers to use garments many times before disposing. Other initiatives include recycling 'old' products back into raw materials and therefore creating 'new'. This reuse is it at the heart of the circular economy.

Risk measures and controls in fashion supply chains

Risk management in the supply chain is a big issue. In a circular economy and sustainable supply chain we must consider environmental risk as a priority alongside the other key supply chain risk issues. Global sourcing and mass production at speed have increased such issues to create a supply chain crisis – the fashion industry is responsible for taking steps to ensure a more sustainable and equitable supply chain. This is where risk management is of paramount importance.

All risks must be considered and identified by those involved in the supply chain, from product development through to manufacturing and distribution, especially in the context of global sourcing. All business involves some degree of risk and the fashion business is no different from any other in this respect, although it should be noted that demand for products in the fashion industry is more unpredictable than in other industries; sales can easily be higher or lower than predicted.

The outsourcing and sub-contracting of manufacturing means retailers can easily lose visibility of the production of goods and raw materials. Retailers are usually located thousands of miles away from their manufacturers or suppliers, which is one of the most difficult areas for risk management. Goods are at risk of being damaged or stolen in transit and additionally, there may be unforeseen delays in delivery due to weather conditions and natural disasters – this can be anything from flooding or snow to severe problems such as earthquakes. Another issue with global sourcing is changes in export or import tariffs and fuel costs and fluctuations in currency rates – all of which affect the cost price of a garment. To negate the impact of these risks it makes sense for retailers to have a spread of different suppliers in different regions as well as the appropriate skill set.

At the product development end of the process it is easy to miss deadlines for production; designs may be misinterpreted by manufacturers or replicated by other retailers who are using the same supplier. Staff turnover can also present risks, particularly within buying, merchandising and design teams. Employees will often move around, sometimes to the competition, and may take information with them: this is difficult to prevent but can be managed.

It is essential for retailers to undertake careful risk assessment and implement a robust risk-management process in SCM. If fashion retailers work with the correct partners and build good relationships in SCM, then they are likely to be more reliable and flexible and implementation of any agreements or process will be much simpler to adhere to. In addition, it is important for a business to review its key performance indicators, which can be used each season to review the effectiveness, reliability, quality, responsiveness and flexibility of partners in the supply chain.

Key performance indicators

A business will often create measures to monitor its performance and that of its suppliers. These measures are known as key performance indicators (KPIs).

KPIs and measures in supply chain

Most fashion businesses will set measures and controls for their strategy and business. These are applied in the supply chain by reviewing efficiency, speed to market, quality and sustainability. These KPIs will also be applied to suppliers, including the logistics operation, in addition to manufacturers. They are usually derived from key objectives of the business.

The importance of sustainability has created measures and controls. There are two important examples:

The Higg Index

A toolset, developed by the Sustainable Apparel Coalition, SCA, allows companies and brands of all sizes to review their sustainability performance by providing them with a measurable score and advises those facilities on how and where they can make improvements. Search online for 'Higg' to find out more about the SCA.

Triple bottom line

A concept first coined by John Elkington in 1994, the triple bottom line consists of the three Ps – profit, people, and planet – by which companies should assess their bottom lines. Profit is the traditional bottom line of finances within corporations. In addition to profit, triple bottom line businesses also measure their performance in terms of social (people) and environmental (planet) responsibility. Therefore, the triple bottom line is a holistic assessment of a company's economic, social and environmental performance over time.

Logistics and outsourcing in the supply chain

To introduce the subject of logistics, which is a vital part of outsourcing in the chain, we must first understand that all organizations and businesses have to move materials: fashion moves all the time. Manufacturers build factories that collect raw materials from suppliers and deliver finished goods. Logistics is the management of the movement of materials between suppliers and customers and the logistics provider is responsible for bringing all the parts together; they are the link in the supply chain.

There are various reasons why retailers and fashion businesses have invested in logistics: these include rising costs, competition and internationalization. There are further opportunities to reduce costs by creating efficient transport and distribution systems. In marketing terms, an effective logistics strategy will enable a retailer to deliver promises to its customers: in other words, goods on time.

Reducing cost

In the supply chain, products should flow as if passing through a pipeline. Stock should be continually moving to keep costs down: in production, in transit, in a container or on a ship, then into a distribution centre and out to stores. Stock that stands still does not add value, only cost.

Logistics has been described as the 'last cost-saving frontier' in a business, creating productivity and value. SCM is now regarded as a key element in customer service and logistics is an important basis for differentiation. The shift to international sourcing and distribution has created further complexity of logistical operations and many retailers and fashion companies will outsource this highly specialized part of the supply chain to companies such as DHL/EXEL. These specialists handle all of the transportation and collection of goods and organize documentation ready for export.

Logistics

A key part of any fashion supply chain relies on its ability to transport finished goods inevitably requiring the services of a third party logistics supplier (3PL).

The main activities of a logistics provider include:

× The procurement or purchasing of raw materials
× Inward-bound transport (such as fabric)
× The receipt of goods
× Warehousing or storage of goods at port, with the manufacturer or in a distribution centre (DC)
× Stock control
× Order picking
× Material handling
× Outward transport (to the port)
× Physical distribution of stock via distribution centres
× Recycling and returns (reverse logistics)
× Location of stock in the chain
× Communication with manufacturers and the retailers

Interview

Liz Leffman, Chair, Clothesource

Liz Leffman and Mike Flanagan set up Clothesource twenty-five years ago when Leffman was originally working for Courtaulds Textiles. It was then, in 1990, that Leffman realized that there were significant manufacturing opportunities in Eastern Europe. Initially, Clothesource made one million school shirts – and have been doing that ever since with their small team in Romania. Realizing that there was a need for sourcing information for the global market, Clothesource began life as a newsletter, which then turned into a report and finally developed into the sourcing analysis service for the apparel industry that it is today.

How have you seen the supply chain change in the last decade?

The main changes in sourcing has been the increase into sourcing from China and Bangladesh garment production whilst many other locations have come and gone such as Vietnam and Cambodia.

After the Rana Plaza disaster in Bangladesh, there has been an impact on the fashion industry. The focus on CSR and an increase of retailers sourcing in the area has had a profound effect and has contributed to improved working conditions – this impact has extended into other countries also.

I saw the changes with both Bulgaria and Romania coming into EU – and okay it is a small, but an important change which especially made sourcing from Romania much easier – it is relatively local and convenient for retailers in the UK/EU to source from Eastern Europe.

What do you consider are the main challenges in sourcing fashion?

One of the biggest challenges is that fashion buyers no longer have as much access to factories and a buyer may never visit where their clothing has been made. This is very challenging and what this means is that the factories don't always understand the buyer and their requirements – and equally the buyer may not understand the factory and its constraints.

There is so much pressure on price – and in the past, there were much closer relationships in garment manufacturing. Everything was more of a discussion and this continued pressure on price can impact quality, so it is a tough call.

How important are good relationships in supply chain outsourcing?

These relationships are essential because there has been a tendency in the sourcing of fashion to just focus on and chase price. But you have to find someone that you can rely on and you need to build these relationships where both partners are in a win-win situation. If too much pressure is placed on the factory and workers, this will lead to compromises being made.

In fashion, as we are no longer working in two distinct seasons we require a constant supply of products. It is essential to create these good relationships so that the suppliers can understand your needs – and everyone is in regular contact. It is crucial to do this as fashion brands want this flow of new constant product in store.

What sort of pressure do you see on fashion retailers and suppliers?

I think in general the success of people like Primark has created major pressure and the risk is in reducing quality as well as price. We seem to have lost a sense of differentiation and in reality, there is a big gap between the big chain stores and the designer brands.

In the middle market, brands such as Next and M&S have really gone after the cheap product and it has created a big problem as they do not know whether they should be more distinctive and stand out with product or just go after the lowest price.

Events such as Black Friday do not help this situation and everyone seems to be losing profit margin. Even retailers such as John Lewis and ASOS in the UK (who are online only) appear to be losing profit – people are not so willing to spend on fashion and thus there is more lowering of price. All of this has resulted in a loss of brand USP and a lack of marketing strategy to stand out and differentiate between fashion retailers and brands.

Do you think customers and retailers are willing to see any increase in prices?

Yes, I do actually. If they see something fantastic that they want they will buy it – but unfortunately we seem to have lost that 'not needing but wanting' fashion products and that all important 'aah' factor in fashion.

How easy or difficult do you think it is for fashion retailers to have complete visibility in the supply chain?

It is quite difficult, however, it is not impossible because you can only rely upon what your supplier is telling you unless you visit them regularly and there is much sub-contracting globally in the fashion business.

Also, visibility issues can extend further than the end manufacturer and into the raw material chain and this is where it can be quite opaque and there is a risk of not conforming to your standards. Cotton originating from say Uzbekistan, for example, can easily leak into the supply chain and many retailers have banned the use of raw material from this location due to sustainability issues although there is some technical genetic testing possible to eradicate this.

Although the level of interest in sustainability and visibility at the retail level is not necessarily always there – plus most customers are not that bothered. Obviously, some brands are very concerned about this, but they know they have that customer interested in the wider issues, these include brands such as Stella McCartney.

Which countries or locations do you see as the future for sourcing?

This is always a very hard question – and the obvious answer is the continent of Africa but I really cannot see any of those countries becoming major fashion supply sources. To be honest there really is still so much capacity and labour available in China – and many manufacturers there could move into even more 'local' satellite countries such as Laos and in SE Asia. I do not think Indian manufacturing is likely to increase further and whilst places such as Myanmar have been attempted as 'new' sources the political and socio economic situation remains challenging.

Do you think manufacturing will ever return to being 'local'?
No. I really do not believe it will, for example in the UK the reason is the relatively low unemployment and plus, it is not such an attractive career proposition for young people.

There is a huge investment in training people required for garment manufacturing added to that it is pretty much a minimum wage industry and at the moment it is not particularly difficult to find work in UK. A lot of people in UK and local manufacturing are in fact from EU or are international migrants.

What do you consider are the key areas of sustainability that fashion retailers should focus on?
There are several key areas here to highlight:

1. Packaging is a good example where retailers need to take more responsibility can become more transparent and all packaging should be recycled and ideally should also be biodegradable.

2. The second one is workforce – Fashion retailers need to be able to demonstrate an understanding of workers and labour throughout their supply chains.

3. Raw materials – much more should be done to recycle textiles and create new from old.

Case Study

Kering Group: Transformation through sustainability

(This case study data is taken from 13th Annual Retail and Luxury Goods Club Conference 'Joining the Dots' at Columbia University New York 2 February 2019, where Marie Claire Daveu, the chief sustainability officer at Kering spoke.)

Sustainability in supply chains

The Kering Group own fashion brands including Balenciaga, Gucci, Saint Laurent, Brioni, and Bottega Veneta to name a few and has recently revealed that it is building the corporate strategy and sustainability strategy around three key elements:

× Care
× Collaborate
× Create

These are the three core elements to Kering's 2025 Sustainability Strategy, focused not only on reducing their resource consumption but also inspired by respecting the individual as they strive toward creating the future of fashion, where luxury and sustainability are synonymous.

Kering knew it needed to create a new business model and this one made absolute sense. They realized that raw materials such as cotton, cashmere and silk are not finite nor exempt from the negative impact of climate change. There are many beautiful materials that can be impacted by changing temperatures but sometimes these problems can drive innovation and stimulate entrepreneurial thinking in textile sourcing. Kering brand customers and especially Gen Z now have these expectations from companies and Kering believes that there is more interest and a push to be resilient from all sides,

4.12 **Kering Press Conference, Paris**
Kering's Chairman and Chief Executive Officer Francois-Henri Pinault, Chief Sustainability Officer and Head of International Institutional Affairs Marie-Claire Daveu and Director Tom Beagent attend a press conference in Paris.

which can also create a better perception by investors.

The big luxury brands are known for setting trends in fashion and lifestyle so Kering feels responsible for pathing the way for sustainable change. This is the strongly held view of M. Pinault, CEO, and his commitment to sustainability has driven the Kering Group initiatives and the social and environmental targets, discussed ahead. Kering believe these will have creative positive outcomes for society. However, this journey is not without its challenges and at Kering they understand that the supply chain is the bedrock of its sustainability strategy.

Solution

The solution that Kering created includes a tool that measures and shows the footprint in the entire supply chain and includes the sourcing of raw materials. Outside the company, programmes have been created that collaborate with communities including the Cashmere supply chain, where there is a strong impact on bio-diversity. The company works closely with Mongolian herders to ensure that the native wildlife is protected and is also involved in a regenerative resin process in local woodlands which helps to restore soil and removes CO_2.

Design

On the design side, Kering provides alternative materials from its laboratory in Italy and the designers and technologists work together to create innovative textiles. This innovation is key to reach the target aim to reduce its global impact on raw materials by 20 percent.

Kering also works closely with start-up fashion brands, as it believes that the entire textile industry needs collaboration and cross-sector co-operation in order for sustainability to become the norm. It believes having designers involved at the laboratory in Novarra near Milan is an essential tactic, as Kering cannot create change without the designers – the ideas come from them. Specifically, the St Laurent and Gucci brands are convinced by the influence of Gen Z and a sustainability strategy.

Future challenges for Kering Group

There are many challenges for a luxury house pursuing sustainability in the next five years, but Kering strongly believes sustainability is not an option for luxury brands, and so has given itself a target to reduce its carbon footprint by 40 percent by 2025.

For example, Kering understands that its global consumers will drive the industry and even influence its choice of supply chains. Kering acknowledges on

4.13 Kering Luxury Goods Group Logo
Kering luxury goods company logo seen displayed on a smartphone. Kering S.A. is an international luxury group based in Paris, France. It owns luxury goods brands including Gucci, Yves Saint Laurent, Balenciaga, Alexander McQueen and Bottega Veneta.

4.14 **Gucci Advert New York**
A Gucci ad is seen displayed
on the wall of a Manhattan
building in New York.
Colossal Media specializes in
hand painted ads in New York
and across the United States.

its website that customers in Asia are asking brands about sustainability issues including transparency of the supply chain and animal welfare, clearly showing the consumers' growing interest in this area.

Kering's view is that the fashion industry as a whole cannot continue as it is and will have to pursue sustainability as a priority also, not as just a trend but as a challenge for the entire industry to face. With that in mind, future strategic initiatives taken should be linked with recycling and upcycling of raw materials and discarded used products. Indeed, recycling fabric and yarn is one of the innovations being developed in the raw materials field and a key starting point for sustainable fashion.

Pricing and sustainability

The Kering Group's view is it can prove sustainability is good for business and sustainability and profit are inextricably linked. The Kering strategic perspective is one of sustainability not just as a cost, but as an investment in the future of its business. Sustainability from the beginning of the process does not cost more and it is important to note that Kering is not merely using sustainability as a way to create a competitive advantage alone. It firmly believes that sustainability is key to protecting its business and ensuring that it can continue for future generations.

'Gen Z (around seven to 23 years old) are a unique force, distinctly different to any previous demographic. As the first generation of true digital natives, technological change, social media, a volatile economic climate and an inherent sense of individualism have reshaped the way they think, communicate and consume.'
– Stylus.com

Chapter summary

This chapter has explored supply chain management (SCM) and its importance to the fashion business and merchandising. Successful companies are those that ensure their staff are well trained and aware of their impact on the supply chain, ensuring that the supply chain is working to its optimum capacity and efficiency. If fashion retailers and businesses get it right, SCM offers huge potential rewards. We are in a challenging yet exciting time for fashion supply chains; many brands have realized that sustainable materials and alternatives need to be considered globally and importantly integrated into large-scale brand supply chains. Although 'fast fashion' is clearly a successful business model and is unlikely to disappear, new initiatives and embedding of sustainability in many fashion supply chains has gained traction. However, it is coming along late in the day and the future of our industry depends on this expansion and a much needed paradigm shift. To protect the environment and those who work in fashion supply chains we need to do more, and continually re-think the business models we use and consider sustainability from cradle to cradle. Look at it as an opportunity to re-invent the way we use precious resources – if you are reading this chapter as you enter the fashion industry then that means YOU.

Questions and discussion points

We have discussed the different issues associated with supply chain management. With this in mind, consider the following questions:

1. Consider a country or region you are familiar with and analyze whether it is in a pre-industrial, industrial or post-industrial stage. What is the main form of employment there: service industry or manufacturing?

2. Who are the biggest fashion retailers in your local shopping area? Do they display country of origin in the clothing sold? Visit several websites of fashion brands, review their CSR policy and compare with the ETI base code.

3. Do any fashion retailers you are familiar with have a code of conduct for suppliers displayed anywhere for customers to see? Investigate two very different brands and find out where they produce their products. How transparent is the information provided?

4. Identify a number of fashion brands and find out where they are manufacturing; do they manufacture in China, Turkey or India? Is there any 'local' manufacturing evident?

5. Identify those designers who are using sustainable practice in their business. Do they promote this?

6. Identify who are the largest global cotton producers and how much of it is fairly traded. Research cotton production in Uzbekistan to understand the issues with the raw material supply chain.

7. Investigate recycling and the circular economy in fashion supply chains. Where do you see examples of best practice? Which brands or retailers are doing a good job? Who are not?

Exercises

We have seen how a continually changing world market presents major challenges for all fashion businesses. Retailers and clothing manufacturers must consider the impact of the supply chain as they continue to develop products and markets overseas. These exercises are designed to help you consider these issues in more detail.

1. Relationships in sourcing and logistics are vitally important. Discuss and review why this is true in global sourcing.

2. You are a buyer for a well-known denim brand. The fabric takes four weeks to produce in bulk and the garments take six weeks to produce, both in India. The shipping by sea to the USA adds another three to four weeks. Your CEO wants these new styles in stores in ten weeks. What can you do to change the lead time? How can you achieve this? What impact will this have on the supply chain? What compromises may need to be made?

3. Consider the impact of the following risks upon supply chains:

   × A 5 percent increase in oil prices
   × A fabric supplier going out of business
   × An earthquake in the country making your goods
   × A lorry being hijacked and losing the contents
   × A designer leaving to join a competitor
   × Delivery of goods is one month late

   Which of these risks, in your opinion, is likely to have the greatest impact on your business and its supply chain? Score them for probability '1–10' and impact '1–10'.

Fashion Brands

This chapter explores some of the more exciting aspects of marketing and branding. It examines some of the intangibles in the fashion business such as customer behaviour, brand identity and extension, brand equity and loyalty. In addition, it discusses advertising, the influencers and the interaction between social media and fashion brands. Finally, it examines a pressing concern for brands today: the scourge of counterfeit goods.

Marketing for fashion is an essential tool for any brand and should be integrated with strategy to reflect key objectives of the brand. The key areas of fashion marketing include customer behaviour, promotion, brand management and value. Brand management should include protection and copyright-IP intellectual property. Fashion marketing has experienced similar levels of digital disruption as the rest of the fashion business; this is most evident in the use of social media, online selling and electronic word of mouth (E-WOM). The advent of 24/7 culture, the instantly 'shoppable' nature of catwalks, impact of 'See Now Buy Now' on consumer spending habits plus the creation of communities reviewing products online has created a completely different landscape.

5.1 The British House, Beijing
Here we can see The British House, a luxury concept store selling many luxury British brands and incorporating a Harrods tea room.

Blogging and sharing information about products via sites such as Instagram is an example where successful marketing for fashion has embraced change. This democratization of the industry has created an instant gratification culture and real time landscape where fashion brands compete globally. Delivering the right message, brand value and story to customers in our hyper-connected world is paramount for successful fashion brand management.

Customer profiling

Customer behaviour can be unpredictable and it is difficult and at times risky to make assumptions about who will buy your brand but it is probably safe to assume that customers can be promiscuous with their purchasing habits and highly sophisticated in terms of taste. Consumers today are affluent, discerning, demanding, cosmopolitan, educated and time-pressured and spoiled for choice. They want it all now and it is a crowded marketplace for fashion brands who need to stand out.

Customer behaviour is related to the rate of consumption and the customer's decision-making process, their wants and needs and their consumer type. In marketing terms, we group consumers into generational cohorts – see the list of key generational cohorts. Regardless of which consumer group a brand is aiming to reach, we should remember we are all in the age of a hyper-connection, meaning that most consumers will have much higher expectations in the digital landscape than ever before. Analyzing shopping behaviour is crucial to a brand's success as it examines the customer's response to the retail experience, choice of store and purchase decision.

Consumption also varies according to changes in society and differential growth in population. Changes in location of groups of customers within countries and sub-regions, in addition to cultural and regional tastes, can all affect consumption patterns within markets.

Consumer types

× Need-driven customers; the activity is driven by need rather than preference. Consumers such as this are price conscious.
× Outer-directed customers form the bulk of the market. These consumers are concerned with status prosperity and getting ahead. They are concerned with products that 'say' something about them.
× Inner-directed customers are few but growing in number. They are more flamboyant and individual; trendsetters from whom ideas diffuse to other groups.

5.2 Ambassadors Unveil 'One Ocean One Planet', Carnaby Street
Ocean Conservation Group 'Project 0' ambassadors unveil 'One Ocean One Planet'. Ambassadors include eco-minded model Pixie Geldof and 'Curiously Conscious' fashion blogger Besma Whayeb.

'Today's consumers are "always on"—better informed, better connected to others, more demanding, and more conscious of values and authenticity. We are seeing a global trend for convenient, on-demand products and services. As an example, there are a few luxury handbag brands that you have to wait a year to receive the product. Whereas now you have companies like Net-a-porter when you can have same day.'
– The Business of Fashion and McKinsey & Company, 2016

Key generational cohorts

Baby boomers 1946-1964: These are often affluent 'older' customers who have high disposable incomes and pensions and are without debt

Gen X 1965-1985: Known as the 'rebellious' generation – growing up in the era of punk rock and protest

Gen Y 1986-1994: Also known as Millennials – a real target for fashion brands. Gucci has its own Millennial committee.

Gen Z 1995-2012: Becoming very attractive to fashion brands as GEN Y become older this group is concerned about the future of the planet and completely immersed in the digital world.

Lifestyle change

There have been ongoing changes in customer lifestyles, including population fluctuation. Population growth in northern Europe has slowed in the last forty years. This is projected to decrease again. The lower birth rates are driven by reduced fertility rates and a change in social attitudes towards working women. For example, in the western world there are far more single households and people living alone; the total number of single households is rising.

This has many different implications, such as singles who have no children to look after and a higher disposable income but are sole breadwinners. The pre-retirement age group are active consumers with free time and money; this is evident in countries such as the UK and USA.

But what does all this mean?

The broad-scale structure of customer consumption will continue to change over time. As income and occupations have changed, so too has expenditure on medical, entertainment, education and cultural activities. All of this creates opportunities and threats for retailers and the development of new service-related product markets. The key to success is to recognize and anticipate consumer change. Differences in customer attitudes and views are crucial to fashion retailers when devising product ranges and retail store formats. Lifestyle changes can create service opportunities but equally may create a shortage of employment in the future.

Positive effects of lifestyle change

- × More women in senior management
- × Inheritance income
- × Adoption of technology in the home has widened customer horizons and contributed towards the increase in travel
- × Changed perceptions of shopping criteria and more options to purchase
- × New product markets
- × Transfer of consumer spending
- × Higher expectations

Building a brand

Customer behaviour and marketing are at the very heart of fashion brands. There can often be a smoke and mirrors approach to advertising and marketing within the fashion business.

Smoke and mirrors may refer to any sort of presentation by which the audience is intended to be deceived, such as an attempt to fool a prospective customer into thinking that one has capabilities necessary to deliver a product in question. Marketing fashion involves continual reinvention and rebranding to attract and entice customers.

Brand building begins with a clear definition of the target customer and the benefits of using a designer name. The advertising and promotion of a fashion brand should reflect an image that can promise customer satisfaction. Brand names are complex and they represent something special to each customer group – it is this combination of tangible and intangible factors that help create a certain image or association in the eye of the customer.

A designer name is usually a vital part of the selling, pricing, promotion and communication strategies; successful designers realize that they are involved in running a business that is a recognizable brand.

Luxury brands

Most brands and fashion retailers are international or global, driven by home market saturation and the need to seek out new opportunities and customers. It is relatively straightforward to achieve, by showing on the runway or online, having a shoppable website and providing global distribution to customers. In expansion terms this may make good strategy but it is fraught with difficulty in terms of understanding a new market. Consumer taste outside of the home territory must be considered in order to succeed; being different is not always sufficient.

International retail can often be a story of failure but, if there is sufficient investment and research into the local market, it can equal success. Luxury goods retailers are experts at this; in combination with big budgets and campaigns the brand can drive success through global expansion whilst mass market brand success is also linked to global domination.

It is important to define what 'luxury' really means, particularly in fashion. A typical traditional luxury consumer is affluent and will appreciate quality, heritage and good value.

For some consumers, luxury goods are very much a symbol of success; buying a luxury product is about displaying the ability to spend large sums of money and define one's status. Luxury means something different to everyone and it is important to outline the market within which the brand operates and then examine what is meant by luxury within that market.

5.3 Chanel Store, Paris
A storefront window of the French fashion house and luxury goods Chanel shop on the Avenue Montaigne in Paris.

'Luxury brands convey unique sociocultural and individual meanings to their consumers. According to Kapferer (1997) these meanings convey their own culture and way of life: hence Saint Laurent is not Chanel. When consumers talk about the affluent lifestyle, they often talk about particular brands. Some of the most prominent examples of this phenomenon would be Rolex watches, Louis Vuitton bags, and jewellery by Tiffany.'
– Yuri Seo, Margo Buchanan-Oliver, 2015

5.4 Luxury Retailer Celine
A craftsman organizes the different components for the manufacture of a Celine handbag at 'La Manufacture', luxury leather goods Celine's new factory in Florence, Italy.

Mass market and fast fashion brands

We have seen emerge through the democratization of fashion so-called 'affordable' high-street luxury. This may be a blended cashmere sweater or a designer collaboration such as Giambatissta Valli at H&M. Exclusivity of the product is important for true luxury which can mean waiting lists for limited editions and customized products such as a Hermes Birkin bag. When we are buying luxury goods we are sometimes buying a little bit of heritage; the DNA of the brand. The price is often irrelevant in true luxury, unlike the mass market where style on a budget but with some exclusive elements as part of marketing campaigns are applied and manifested through celebrity and designer collaborations.

International brands such as H&M, Zara and UNIQLO tend to be successful, for example in the case of Zara, who become the worlds largest fashion retailer with its footprint in every large city. Success and internationalization often go hand in hand with scale and the economies of that scale plus successful distribution and efficient supply chain models (See Chapter 4). Equally 'online' and 'offline' sales are crucial to this success and is linked to having the correct supply chain and logistics in place to meet orders.

There has been a blurring of business models between luxury and mass market as the mass market aims for 'masstige' mimicking the luxury brand premium products. Meanwhile, the luxury market mimicks the mass market by creating 'new product drops' and working with popular celebrity culture and influencers to market its products. The 'streetwear' and 'athleisure' trends are evident at all levels of the fashion market.

Success factors for international brands

The digital landscape means most brands have the ability to be international. The 'born global' concept of fashion brand creation is driven by online and the advent of marketplace selling via such sites as Farfetch, Zalando, Amazon and many others have enabled this trend.

A successful brand adapts quickly to market pressures and has the capacity to produce collaborations and new lines, such as diffusion or bridge lines. Controlling costs is also crucial to good brand management. This does not necessarily mean goods should be cheap; rather, they should be good value – every stage in the product development process needs to add value to the brand.

Focus is important to brands and so is the legitimacy or authenticity of the brand. The luxury goods market was initially slow to embrace social media and online retailing but it has more than made up for this. One only needs look at Oliver Rousteing at Balmain and his use of social media and the so-called 'Oliver's Army' of Instagrammers and influencers has created a new audience and helped increase the brand awareness.

Brand extensions such as cosmetic and perfume ranges, eyewear or leather goods have historically been areas that can help build brands, help to spread the name and increase profit. However, over-diversification and brand extension via licensing can cheapen and weaken a brand if not strictly controlled. This is why many luxury brands will not go down this route unless they spend time and effort investing in manufacturing and the supply chain. A key factor for luxury brands is control over its manufacturing and supply chain and, of course, the brand itself (see Chapter 4: The Supply Chain).

Brand extension and layering

Brand extension and building is a lengthy process. It is essential to ask some key questions before a new range or product is developed, such as:

× Have we exhausted opportunities to grow in the existing market segment

× If not, would this not be lower risk and quicker?

× Are we going to be distracted from the core business?

× Does our brand image 'fit' with the new products or new market?

× Will we still have economies of scale in the global market?

× Can we compete in the 'new' market with the existing competition?

Brands are continuously thinking of new and original ways to meet customers' needs. American fashion brands are expert at brand extension and many pioneered the creation of sub-brands. In the case of a brand such as Ralph Lauren, the brand message is layered to create ranges of affordable luxury.

5.5 Designer Oliver Rousteing
Fashion designer Olivier Rousteing walks the runway during the Balmain Ready to Wear Spring/
Summer 2020 fashion show as part of Paris Fashion Week.

These include diffusion and bridge lines, accessories and home wear ranges. However, brand layering is not an easy strategy for any brand and can lead to a proliferation of brands and labels from certain companies. As a business model this has been replicated by many from the mass market across all market segments including H&M and Zara who both have home wear, childrens' wear, fragrance and accessories. Of course, H&M are well known for co-branding and designer collaborations some of which include Versace, Moschino, Jimmy Choo and other limited edition 'designer' brand collections.

Brand value

The measurement of a brand and its value can determine the brand equity via image, reputation and loyalty. These are intangible qualities, and are difficult to measure, but can create great value for a brand. For example, a brand reputation can be built via the head or creative designer. Their reputation can make a difference to the brand image and therefore help to build brand equity. Other well-known, influential, creative heads of design at large and international luxury brands include Virgil Abloh at Louis Vuitton and Alessandro Michele at Gucci,

5.6 Rag & Bone Brand
A model walks the runway for Rag & Bone during New York Fashion Week showing casual 'athleisure' wear products.

and Riccardo Tisci at Burberry. These designers can help a brand assume value, both financially and in the eyes of the customer. The brand name can be one of the most valuable assets for a fashion business. The creative heads can ensure they keep the brand alive in the minds of the customers and equally help to shape and develop ongoing reputation and success. However, these names and individuals often move from brand to brand which may add another dimension of the brand value discussion and form a part of the continually shifting sands of talent in the fashion sphere.

5.7 AIDA

Customers go through certain key stages when making or considering purchases. The AIDA model is one often used in marketing to highlight the four key stages of a purchasing decision: awareness, interest, desire and action, which is the main aim of brands for their customers to attract and stimulate customers interest and ultimately to make a purchase from their brand offer. An effective brand communication strategy considers the effect on one or all of these stages.

Brand communications

Many retailers create marketing and retail environments to enhance their products. Sportswear brands are very good at this. If we consider Nike and Adidas, the sportswear industry has blended the world of fashion and music, for example, Beyonce's Ivy Park collaboration. This has also contributed to the rise of 'Athleisure' as a key fashion trend.

Consider brands that are easily identifiable thanks to their logos; those that promote an almost 'symbolic' value to customers. This symbolism is part of 'semiotics' and creates an important message sent out by brands. Such symbolism is used by marketers to send subtle messages to customers.

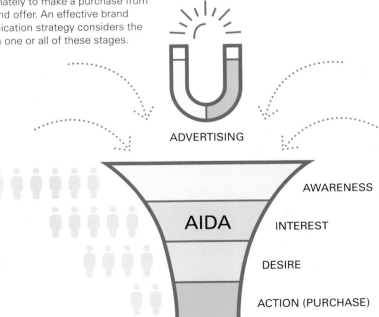

ADVERTISING

AIDA

AWARENESS

INTEREST

DESIRE

ACTION (PURCHASE)

Storytelling and brand promotion

The traditional fashion press has been replaced by social media and online communities that create 'hype' to shape and move brands campaigns and sell products. The big designer brands and fashion houses spend millions of dollars on campaigns; in addition, they use celebrities to promote their products. Such design houses forge close relationships with the fashion press and relevant bloggers and influencers – often referred to as key opinionl (KOLs) – and use of social media channels. Well-known fashion magazines such as *Vogue* and *Bazaar* have paywalls included on their online platforms which means that the access to its content requires subscription by users. In fact, influencers with large followings on social media are also creating 'paywalls' to charge fans for exclusive content on Instagram stories.

Fashion brands must connect with their customers and these connections can be most powerful through the use of digital 'storytelling'. Thanks to the expanding reach of social media, companies can successfully communicate their brand's ethos, values and key facets, and bring their whole brand to life through their online presence. Social media and websites communicate these essential brand messages through their content, providing new stories and up-to-date information for customers to consume. There are some excellent examples of fashion brands who tell 'stories' through campaigns such as Kate Spade, whose campaigns have won a Cannes Lion award for its video content. Social media channels are by far the most important form of communication for brands to send effective relevant messages to their customers. Personalizing content and messages based on consumer purchasing behaviour is an important element for fashion brands to consider. It is especially important for up-and-coming brands to create this online presence through storytelling to build customer awareness of the brand.

'Development of an authentic message a system of beliefs and higher values, in today's market is critical. If you have no story behind the product, you cannot engage emotionally. It doesn't matter how amazing your collection is, if there is no inbuilt integrity, then any initial brand success will probably be short-lived.'
– Joanne Yulan Jong, 2018

5.8 Street Style in Berlin
In this image we see Ines Rovira wearing cycle pants and a leather jacket and Alba Miro wearing an orange bag, asymmetrical sneakers and a wool coat, seen at Bread&Butter Trade Fair by Zalando, Berlin, Germany.

Brand promotion

Big brands spend millions of dollars on campaigns. These can also include events, in-store events, catwalks and use of celebrities. Recent notable campaigns include the Louis Vuitton diversity campaign under the direction of Virgil Abloh with the use of high-profile photographers and themes around minority groups and issues and with references back to art and painters such as Gustave Courbet.

Promotion in the fashion business

PR and promotion is an extremely important tool in the industry, invaluable for building good relationships between the brand and the media. Instagram, Facebook, Snapchat and Twitter offer great PR communication tools for fashion brands and have the potential to increase links with the customer and make them feel more 'connected' to the brand.

Celebrity culture

Many customers are influenced by celebrity culture and, in turn, celebrities' wardrobes. Instagram, Facebook and reality TV, plus the wealth of specialist magazines available, have a huge influence upon customer spending and tastes. Good PR managers understand the benefit of certain individuals who are in the spotlight wearing designer labels. Many fashion houses now use celebrities in their advertising campaigns to enhance brand equity, ensuring that customers stay connected to the brand. Indeed, many celebrities such as Rihanna and Kanye West have their own fashion brands driven by the success of celebrity culture. Rihanna launched her in-house luxury brand 'Fenty' through LVMH group, becoming the first celebrity to launch a new luxury brand at LVMH.

Brand protection

One of the downsides of mass-market production is the illegal copying of designer products and a developing black market industry of counterfeit goods. Customers want to see logos and certain brands in particular have emblazoned their products with a name or label, which has in effect contributed to the problem. It is difficult to prevent replication of products in an industry that thrives on trends and ideas and this problem has, to some extent, been driven by the international success and reputation of some brands.

It is not just the luxury sector that suffers: in the mass market the lines between copying and selecting similar themes are extremely blurred. Fashion designers are often working on similar themes and have access to the same sources of inspiration and trends that are used as part of the range-planning process.

Low-cost retailers are certainly capable of undercutting the mid-market stores by using cheap foreign labour and inferior materials – and by copying original designs.

One way that designers and brands can protect themselves is by trademarking their work and registering the logo and labels as their work. It should be a symbol of quality and authenticity. But high-street copies are much more difficult to protect – it is about design integrity and identity and is therefore much more intangible.

5.9 Counterfeit Goods Seller
A fake 'Louis Vuitton' handbag, which has been found as part of an illegal shipment. Luxury brands trawl the world and employ teams of lawyers to track down such items to protect their brand.

'It is worth noting that fashion is a practice that relies heavily on inspiration. In fact, the entire fashion industry is based on the ebb and flow of inspiration and facilitation of trends. It is important to call attention to the distinction between imitation and inspiration. Imitation refers to the production of identical copies and/or the substantial copying other artistic works.'
– Thefashionlaw.com, 2018

Taking steps

There are several organizations that designers can join in order to protect themselves and their products from replication. There are several luxury brand associations used to maintain integrity and to protect and promote luxury brands. In the UK, there is an organization called The Walpole Group, which provides a community for the exchange of best practice ideas to drive business development in the UK and its export markets.

In France, a similar group is the prestigious Comite Colbert, of which many luxury brands such as Chanel, Dior, YSL, Hermès Balmain and Louis Vuitton are members. It acts in a similar fashion to Walpole in that it promotes its members and additionally encourages new French craftsmanship-led brands to flourish in a mass-produced world. It raises the global profiles of these renowned and iconic brands.

From a pure brand-protection perspective ACID is a group especially for designers to register with and obtain information on registering their brands and designs.

The Counterfeit Museum in Paris displays genuine articles, such as luxury items, pharmaceutical products, computer software, spare car parts and tobacco, alongside their counterfeit copies to demonstrate the differences between the original and the fake.

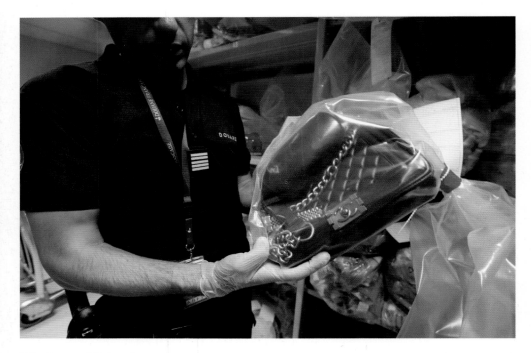

5.10 Counterfeit Goods
A police officer is holding a seized fake 'Chanel' handbag in France.

Interview

Paul Alger, Director of International Business, UK fashion and textiles organization (UKFT)

Paul has been in fashion and textiles for almost thirty years, although he still considers himself to be the 'new boy on the block'. At the UKFT, Paul Alger's role is primarily international business, but as we are in a global industry and in order to teach companies, designers, brands and manufacturers how to export the UKFT feels it is essential to teach them how to trade closer to home in addition to going overseas. Fashion remains a global industry and UKFT looks outwards by selling to the USA, Japan, the EU as their top three markets. The UKFT covers as many markets as it feels the UK fashion industry wants. It also works with a textile consultant based in Yorkshire as a national trade association and with companies throughout all the regions of the UK.

Which brands do you consider currently are most influential in the global market?

In the UK we have a number of very well-known brands that for us at the UKFT are instrumental when we target new markets. So, for example, when we wanted to enter Chinese and Russian markets we looked at what Paul Smith and Vivienne Westwood were doing there – and I took the view that if they were not present in the 'new' market then it would be very difficult for other British brands to enter those new markets without these names being present.

Big names provide the cultural reference point by which large parts of the industry is judged. We could add people such as Stella McCartney, Jenny Packham, Hussein Chalayan and Mary Katrantzou to this list. Also, interestingly looking at the more international 'brands' (depending on the definition of the word) we can add such names as Ted Baker and Reiss, Fred Perry. The UKFT work with many smaller start-up brands and not just large brands.

There are some very interesting niche brands in the UK that are successful such as Ally Cappellino who has been going for a long time and Margaret Howell and although they may not be well known in the UK by Joe Public, they are very well known in Japan. So, because the UK market is dysfunctional to a certain degree (and in my view, we do not support our own brands enough at the consumer level and that is a challenge we face as an industry) plus the Japanese really understand the Margaret Howell brand and are willing to pay a premium for UK manufacturing and ethically made product as that is important to them. We have a number of global British brands not that well known in UK such as Jeff Griffin of Griffin Laundry and Nigel Cabourn that are popular in Japan and these companies develop products by working very closely with UK manufacturers. People like Symonds who make beautiful leather crafted coats made in UK are items that internationally sought after.

Who are the new movers and shakers?

It is worth us mentioning China again, it is a market which has been a long-term target for the UKFT and we have been working there in the last 6–7 years supported by the British Consulate in Shanghai it has become a major growth market. We were very ahead of our time and others have followed us, helped in some way by the research we have conducted in that region. The ethnic Chinese designers have come through strongly learning from education and fashion design and many choose to base their businesses in the UK and are attracted by the ease of coming here to learn from our world class fashion design and education in our Universities. A number of these are very important at Paris fashion week, such as, Xu Zhi (Daniel Chen), Haizhen Wang, Huishan Zhang and Steven Tai.

These brands are very well known as Chinese designers, but are based in the UK. What is exciting to us as an industry about these companies is that they choose to be in the UK and also work very strongly in China. So, effectively these designers act as a bridge between here and China. Also, most are passionately determined to keep some manufacturing in the UK and are effectively selling Chinese taste on British fashion design which makes it quite unusual and very quirky.

I would suggest there is not much of this activity in Italy or France so we are very keen to see this trend with Chinese designers continue and develop and I know academia and our colleagues at the British Fashion Council also want this to continue as it helps the future of our industry. One of the things I am most excited about in this industry is that the UK is a melting pot and a very open society that welcomes people who want to stay here and run their businesses and pay taxes and contribute to society as a whole.

What changes do you notice in customer behaviour?

The customer is king! And although the customer has been king for a long time the change in recent times is the consumer has decided to make their decisions based on opinions from taste makers and fashion journalists.

What has really changed for us is the influencers via the advent of Social Media in the fashion business particularly Facebook, Instagram, Twitter and of course WeChat in China and Line in Japan. These channels have revolutionized the fashion industry, they put designers directly in touch with customers and this has created opportunities, it gives small brands the opportunity to engage directly with customers and talk to them and use that communication as a sales tool.

Instagram is the most popular channel used and we see many designer brand businesses also using Facebook to create a community around a product or idea so the retailers and the press influence has considerably weakened. The celebrity influence on brands has its pluses and minuses in our society, but from a designer point of view it means that if a buyer from a large store will not engage with the fashion brand collection then the designers have the ability to sell their brand directly. This is very much the same as in publishing and is part of the democratisation of the fashion industry.

The small independent boutiques in the UK are interesting, and remain strong, contrary to public opinion the big department stores do not give designers their first break. It is often retailers such as Browns and the Tim Everest (who has a new store in the East End of London). The independent stores are small swift and nimble and have the ability to cope with fast change. As an organization, the UKFT has tended to push our designers to export as a tactic because we realize that if they can become successful in Japan then ironically the UK retailers will then want to sell the brand.

What differences have you noted over the last two years in brand loyalty and consumer purchasing behaviour?
Consumer purchasing behaviour is key because the customer being king makes that possible and also means small designers can sell directly to customers, but there are two big challenges -one is the increasing cost of real estate space which pushes them out of the market. The second is what I often refer to as the 'tyranny of customers'due to online retailing. The customers have a *'give us this product now, not tomorrow at a price that is the lowest one we can possibly get and is also cheaper than last year'*. Previously fashion retailers were able to explain that the experience of going into a store had high cost attached to it, but now the customer wants all of the trappings of the store but with the online price.

There is a race to bottom in the fashion business which is not sustainable, with many retailers putting huge amount of pressure on suppliers. We live in a world of scarce resources and retailers cannot all their pass price increases to consumer.

At some point customers' will have to accept this fact – the consumer needs to be made aware that there is more than just a financial cost to making products in locations such as Bangladesh.

How do you see the future of bricks and mortar retailers?
I think bricks and mortar need to think about how they remain relevant in the twenty-first century and I know a number of retailers are looking at the total 'experience' of that juxtaposition of 'going out shopping' rather than walking up and down Oxford Street looking for a bargain. The 'let's go out and spend some quality time' element part of the experience needs to be made obvious by retailers.

We also need to give overseas consumers coming to the UK something special and I hope that retailers will look more at local UK manufacturing so customers can then take something home that has meaning, a good example is Selfridges who are now working with and selling the smaller UK brands.

How does the strategy of luxury brands differ from the mainstream brands?
The fashion industry is undergoing a huge change, even fifteen years ago I was working with beautiful luxury handbag makers who were struggling to make their product in same factory as Goyard and Mulberry but were more expensive. Customers can buy luxury direct or from platforms such as Matches and Farfetch but one of the challenges is that many of the international luxury brands sold are Italian or French and only one or two are British – Burberry is, of course, one of these. We have a lot of luxurious

brands and products in the UK and I become quite frustrated as they are so beautiful – yet many consumers never get to see them. They are developing in our ecosystem in the UK working with UK manufacturers and coming out of great Universities using beautiful high quality materials.

Brand equity and loyalty: how can brands change strategy and direction and continue to build and strengthen the brand and keep/increase customers?
It really is a big challenge. There are more and more new designers but we do not have the same type of big retailers these days and companies are finding that they have so much to do running their own on line brand, own social media, press PR and celebrity but at same time they have to run a wholesale sale business.

I think we are on the cusp of another paradigm shift, some designer brands are pulling out of wholesale and investing in brick and mortar. The smaller brands start off online but if they start to grow they need to sell to big companies such as Lane Crawford in Hong Kong and stores in the Middle East, and to compete they need to be able to wholesale. The wholesale model is still very important internationally – the difference is that we live in a 'see it now buy it now' world.

What is your view on the activity of copying or 'passing off' on the high street and also that of counterfeit goods? What can be done about it?
Unfortunately, it is a part of the industry and many companies struggle with this from a commercial perspective. Some brands say when they are doing research

into the Chinese market that their 'brand' was already there under a 'cabbage' arrangement – this is rife in our industry. These brands are already being sold in China and people have already registered their IP in China. These are trademark squatters but the fact is that attitudes to IP in Asia (even in Japan) and not just China are very different from the UK/EU.

Ultimately unless you have a lot of money for expensive lawyers – you are sending good money after bad if you try to sue them. Most designers are so creative they just say it's a compliment – more of an issue is copying on the high-street level in the UK. I recall seeing a sign at Bread and Butter in Berlin saying that no one from Zara, H&M or C&A would be allowed in because they felt they were being copied. The mass market and high street have taken 'inspiration' such as this for years and 7–8 years ago Vivienne Westwood took her inspiration from 'the street'.

But at times the high street take inspiration in a way that is not really fair and an enterprising person at one of the high-street retailers can transform an idea and make it their own and a designer with fantastic idea will lose everything. These retailers ought to think very carefully about being inspired by such designers.

On an export trip to Japan we found three garment versions in the shop of a British designer. The first version was a blatant iteration that had been bought on wholesale basis in Paris, the second was a Chinese fake brand that had seen the collection and been inspired by the original and copied it. The third version was, in fact, unique to Japan; they had taken an element of the garment as it was a best seller – turned it into their own original brand by having had it made in a lighter fabric for summer. Some parts of the world just do not see this as plagiarism but is the main reason more and more retailers have decided to develop their own collection with their own brands to make more profit and control the designs.

There are many trade organisations such as UKFT and the BFC – how can these assist brands and are there similar global organizations you could mention?
There is a lot of support in the UK and there is a lot of help but not a lot of cash, lots of support is via the British Fashion Council. Many universities themselves are supportive of students for example; Central St Martins and the University of Westminster have mentoring support and also lots of start-up brands work with UKFT RISE. Outside the UK there are similar organizations in Europe including: Federation de la Haute Couture et de la Mode, Sisteme a la Moda Italia VDMD – Association of German Fashion and Textile Designers, and ACFDA in the USA.

Additionally, many trade fairs and exhibitions offer outreach to brands internationally. The UK Luxury goods group Walpole are very interesting and are very exclusive at a certain level unlike the UKFT which is more is inclusive. There are also a couple of online bloggers such as 'Grey Fox' who have created a network around themselves.

How do you see the format for the future for retailing, particularly fashion brands?
I think it is difficult to see how the future for retail will go at present, but I do think that fashion retail needs to become fun again – I am saying this as a consumer frustrated at the moment in addition to being an industry professional. I want to be excited and find unique product when I go out to look for it. The UK is unlike Japan or Italy where there are some amazing independent boutiques. I hope we can somehow re-create that independent model in fashion retail again. Customers need to find interesting stores we can buy interesting new product from in the provincial cities and not just in London.

Case Study
The British House, TBH Beijing

(Taken from interview with Jamie Powell by the author and reference to the website.)

The British House (TBH) was opened in 2017 and is a showcase for British Brands in Beijing. It is a luxury concept store covering lifestyle food, fashion and all things British for the discerning Chinese market. It sells over 100 British luxury brands, and is home to the first Harrods tea room in China. It was established by TBH Founder Yimei McCabe. This case study is based on an interview with Jamie Powell who is the TBH retail director in addition to managing the TBH website. Jamie's career spans thirty years in the industry – he began his career at Harrods as a management trainee working in all areas including supply chain, logistics and the shop floor.

Jamie Powell then set up Hunters of Brora Cashmere with the owners' daughter. Jamie then went to work for Giorgio Armani in Hong Kong, French Connection, Fila in Milan and Burberry in London. He has also worked for Hickey Freeman and acted as a consultant to brands such as Ede & Ravenscroft and was also the CEO of Jonathan Saunders.

5.11 Retail Area of the British House
A view of one of the floors inside The British House Store in Beijing, China.

5.12 The British House
The VIP room in The British House in Beijing, China.

The store

TBH flagship store in Beijing was selected as the premier location for TBH because Beijing is the capital and the location is iconic, being on the corner of Tiananmen Square which is an area built on ring roads in the dead centre of Beijing. The opportunity to open TBH in such an iconic area made it a relatively easy decision for the owner. TBH is located in between two 150-year-old buildings in this historic Chinese government-owned area and had to be approved by the government to open there. It is a magnificent area of Beijing for visitors and shoppers alike.

History of TBH

Before establishing The British House, the owner of TBH, Mrs Yimei McCabe, helped the Chinese launches of brands including Hugo Boss and Alfred Dunhill and also set up the 'Highgrove' Brand belonging to HRH The Prince of Wales in 2010 in China. Yimei ran this for four years and it is a B2B business rather than C2C so her idea was to develop the C2C concept further, as the Highgrove brand was being sold by several large upscale retailers in China.

Product mix

When it came to making decisions about the important product and brand mix positioning, the TBH team, headed by Jamie Powell, focussed on how they could develop the range of Highgrove products further and expand incrementally into other heritage brands. The positioning of these brands needed to match closely to the Harrods brands in London. The

Highgrove brand position was at a certain level and a priority was to have a tea room to drive traffic.

The product selection and adjacencies of the brands was a very important element of the selection-making process. So that they could maintain the same quality of brands the team focussed on other Royal Warrant brands including premier British examples such as Johnstons of Elgin, John Smedley, a 200-plus-years-old brand, and other beautiful quality cashmere brands. Some of the top selling brands in TBH are the Harrods tea room (with its own pantry and products for sale) plus Highgrove across all its product sectors and Joshua Ellis Cashmere and Cambridge satchel company. Of course, TBH is very discreet about revealing any actual sales figures of its brands and

it is important to note TBH does not stock international Bond Street brands that are already widely available in China but instead much more traditional British brands such as those found on Jermyn Street.

Customers

TBH management team expected the customer demographic to be aged to be 45-plus (due to the product mix and the positioning) but realized quite quickly that actual customers were younger business professionals 25–45 years old. These were people who had studied internationally and worked in professional roles; senior executives in middle management with young families and children, which as a market was much more appealing for some of TBH younger brands.

5.13 **Retail Area of the British House**
A floor showing menswear in The British House in Beijing, China.

This group of customers in China love things that are British as they remind them of the UK. It should be noted there are over 650,000 alumni of British universities and around 65,000 anglophiles in Beijing. Chinese TBH customers love to read about brands and are very discerning and interested in the history and where a product originates. They enjoy reading about where the yarn is made and where the buttons are from and will talk on WeChat about a brand history and heritage. There is a real thirst for knowledge from this group who want to see pictures and videos of the manufacturing, so TBH have to continually ask the brands about the story and brands history. In the UK, we might provide customers with around three sentences about a brand by comparison.

Interestingly, children's wear has become a very popular range for customers of TBH who usually have children of around 5–12 years old and this popularity is partly due to the influence of HRH Prince William and his wife the Duchess of Cambridge in China. There are thirty brands in total and TBH did look at a slightly lower-priced mix of children's brands but also wanted to include ones with strong heritage and history to create a 'mini' TBH feel to the product offer to match those of its men's and women's wear ranges.

Customer service
Beijing is much more discreet as a city than Shanghai. It is a city far more used to having trendy brands since the 1920s and known as 'little Paris'. Beijing is much less 'flashy' and in addition to conservative society there has been a government clampdown on an ostentatious gifting culture. People in Beijing are generally much more conservative and customers look for brands that are more exclusive and low key than those they may find in Shanghai. TBH delivers anywhere in China within fourteen days.

Locational strategy
TBH have just signed a contract to open a new store in Tianjin city which is based on the sea and is an international city with European architecture and a population of 16 million, plus there is a bullet train service to Beijing which only takes forty minutes. TBH are considering a number of other sites in China and in Asia including Macau, Hong Kong and Singapore and also considering opportunities in the Middle East but these are still under discussion with the partners. There is a store opening rollout plan for China and other Tier1 and Tier 2 cities such as Shanghai and Shenzhen. TBH aims to create a bespoke mix of products for each store and intends to tailor this mix to the local need and customer preferences.

Competition
The obvious competition in China is 'Lane Crawford' which is a Hong Kong–based 100-year-old department store covering multiple sites in China. There is some crossover with TBH British Brands, although TBH considers everyone to be a potential competitor and good pricing to be important even for luxury and heritage brands. TBH offers an incubation opportunity for new young brands and helps to promote new brands in the marketplace but in Beijing there are French and Japanese brands to compete with too. TBH considers part of their USP to offer education through in-store events featuring music and art (working closely with universities) which help to drive its own special niche in the market, and it is a very important aspect of its strategy for the brand.

5.14 The British House
The exterior of The British House, which is located in between two 150-year-old buildings in an historic Chinese government-owned area of Beijing, China.

Marketing

The marketing strategy in Asia is very different from the West; there is little of the 'magazine culture' and everything is done through all social media using various platforms including WeChat. An important aspect of the TBH marketing strategy is that it reaches out to its high-net-worth individual clients and also runs a lot of private parties for these clients providing them with exclusive opportunities to discreetly view items such as jewellery and watches. These events are invite only and it is a way for this group of customers to attend a private lunch or have cocktails, for example, with an ambassador from the UK. TBH also provides exclusive trunk shows and private fashion shows to make the more discerning customer feel special and provide them with the ability to spend in a more private and discreet manner.

Chapter summary

Chapter 5 has examined some of the intangibles in the fashion business such as brand identity and extension, equity and loyalty. It looked at the influence of social media and storytelling as tools, and the interaction with designers and brands, and how the promotion of a fashion brand should reflect an image for consumers to identify with. A brand needs to have a USP – a unique selling point. This is most difficult to achieve in the crowded, switched-on fashion market. Finally, we examined the ways in which copying and counterfeiting can affect fashion brands.

Questions and discussion points

We discussed brand identity and extension, brand equity and the issues with counterfeit goods. With this in mind, consider the following questions:

1. How many brands can you think of that are widely copied and where have you seen copies or counterfeits sold?
2. Consider three designer brands and compare and contrast them. How many ranges or bridge lines do they have?
3. Think about brands that you consider to be new or up-and-coming in your region: why do you think they are becoming popular?
4. How do you think luxury brands stay in control of the brand and product?
5. Which brands do you not have access to that you would like to see in your local area? Why? What is special about them?

Exercises

Brand value can be established via image, reputation and loyalty. These are intangible qualities that are difficult to measure but can create great value for a brand. The following exercises will help you to consider brand value in more detail:

1. Visit three different designer brands, preferably online and stand-alone stores. What differences do you see? Consider the following: product; price; visual merchandising.
2. Look at Instagram and consider its use by different fashion brands; then compare it with another site such as Facebook. What similarities and differences are there?
3. Customers and their shopping habits: visit your nearest shopping mall or high street in a large town or city. Observe the following:
   × Who is shopping there?
   × What age are they?
   × Are they fashionably dressed?
   × Speak to a few customers if possible and find out why they are shopping, for example, is it a special occasion, retail therapy, work and basics or for a replacement product? Are they just browsing and will they then go home and buy online?
4. Consider three luxury brands and compare and contrast the following:
   × History
   × Products
   × Price ranges
   × Store
   × Creative designer

Put together a presentation showing the three that you selected and explain the preceding points using a visual format.

This is a book about the fashion business. At the time of writing, we are going through yet another period of considerable global change brought about by the COVID-19 pandemic. All business, including fashion, is being impacted by this and the likely sustained change will result in what is highly disruptive innovation. We have discussed in this book how globalization is responsible for the development of the industry and that speed of innovation will not cease. It is likely that this will affect supply chains through the further consolidation of designers, retailers and manufacturers, forming close relationships to develop and innovate commercial garments, but new collaborations need to be formed. However, the industry needs to change – sustainability and reuse and recycling of all raw materials and products is urgently required.

Customers may potentially begin to gradually buy better and buy less as a result of this difficult period. Customers are reviewing their outlook and spending habits are inevitably impacted by any global crisis. Shopping is principally still a leisure activity and fashion retailers and brands should not lose sight of that. Fashion is also a commodity and fulfils a need but those brands and fashion retailers prepared to go further – those who can react well and flexibly to change and with a strong USP and innovative products – will be the winners. A solid business model will ensure success, with those who take calculated risks gaining competitive advantage. Essentially, fashion will always be driven by the desire for the 'must-have' as well as fulfilling a need. We have learned that the generic fashion cycle remains constant through the evolution of business trends and macro environments, it is now a circular process while the ongoing analysis of the position and the environment of a fashion business is crucial to future success. We have learned about the importance to stay ahead of key directions and emerging trends. That will always be the case. However, virtual reality may well become the new way of doing business from catwalk shows to selling fashion – retailers will hold less stock and those that succeed will provide technology for customers to engage with products through artificial intelligence.

New roles and responsibilities in the fashion business will continue to evolve. There are many training opportunities worldwide in colleges and universities for designers, buyers, merchandisers and technologists and the new roles stemming from the digital environment. To feed the growing industry it is important to consider the new type of roles and training needed in the future of fashion business; to nurture the talent coming through. Collaboration via acquisitions and mergers in fashion retail is likely to accelerate even further as a result of these environmental and global challenges, whichcan only be a good thing for the sustainability of our industry. At the other end of the scale, there is always demand for individuality in the industry, leading to the rise of niche, original fashion brands. We only need look at the endurance of vintage fashion and the popularity of bespoke goods to see that not all customers seek out mass duplication and proliferation of similar fashion products.

We must never lose sight of creativity in the fashion design and textile process: the application of digitization and technology should aid the process and not be seen as a total replacement for talent, skill, authenticity and true craftsmanship. Fashion has and always will thrive on originality and flair; it offers people the opportunity to stand out from the crowd. Designers and fashion businesses are continually challenged to capture the all-important zeitgeist, and the constant turnover of new ideas that keeps fashion moving.

AIDA model Attention, Interest, Desire and Action.

Baby boomers Those born after the second world war when birth rates rose dramatically; a generational cohort.

Bespoke Made to measure.

Bridge lines Similar to diffusion lines; mid-price ranges cheaper than the main line.

CAD Computer aided design.

CFDA Council for Designers of America.

Comparative shopping Shopping as analysis of the competition.

Concessions Shop within a shop such as a brand in a department store.

Cool hunters Marketing professionals who observe and predict forthcoming and existing cultural trends.

CPFR Collaborative Planning, Forecasting and Replenishment.

CRM Cause related marketing – collaboration between business and not-for-profit organization such as charity.

CSR Corporate Social Responsibility – self regulation of a business within legal ethical and international standards.

DC Distribution centre or warehouse.

Design brief Used by a design team and shared across business functions such as buying.

Direct supply Supply of goods directly from factory to retailer.

Drop model Technique used by retailers to bring new product, often limited editions, into stores.

E-commerce The online sale of goods.

EDI Electronic Data Interchange: the electronic transmission of data between organizations.

EPOS Electronic point of sale.

ETI Ethical trade initiative: an alliance of companies, trade unions and voluntary organizations.

Fast fashion High-street interpretation of designer trends produced using a short supply chain model.

FOB Freight on board: this specifies whether the buyer or seller pays for the shipment and loading costs and at which point responsibility for the goods is transferred.

FSV Full service vendor: a company that takes an active design role and all responsibility for manufacturing and logistics.

Generation X The generation born after the post-World War II baby boom, from the 1960s through to the early 1980s.

Generational cohort A term used in demographic profiling, a generational cohort is a group of individuals who share the experience of common historical events; these include Gen X, Gen Z, Gen Y and Baby boomers.

Good, better, best A pricing matrix used by retailers when planning ranges.

Haute couture Bespoke high fashion.

Key pieces Must-have items within a seasonal range.

Megatrends Macro environmental trends.

MFA Multi Fibre Arrangement: established in 1974 to govern world trade in textiles and garments. It expired on 1 January 2005.

Micro trend Fashion trend that is usually not much more than a fad; lasts weeks not months.

Mood boards Initial design ideas in a visual format, used in the design and range-planning process.

Multi-channel retailer Company that sells its goods through various formats, such as online and bricks-and-mortar stores.

NGO Non-governmental organization: a not-for-profit organization that operates independently from any government.

OPP Opening price point: a retail promotion strategy used to lure customers in.

OTB Open to buy: a flexible budget strategy that enables merchandise to be ordered later on in a buying season.

Outlet Discount malls selling designer end-of-lines or made-for-outlet products.

Own brands Retailers' brands designed in-house. Also known as private label.

PESTEL Political, economic, sociological, technological, environmental and legal analysis: a framework for the macro environment.

Pop-up shop Short-term outlet used by brands to trial a location.

PR Public relations: the practice of promoting public image of an organization or an individual using topics of interest and news items that provide a third-party endorsement and do not direct payment.

Prêt-à-porter Ready-to-wear designer fashion.

Private Label Retailer own brand.

Product development The development of initial ideas into actual garments.

Product mix Based upon the marketing mix and part of range planning.

QR Quick response: a manufacturing model developed by the Japanese, the basis of a fast-fashion supply chain.

Range planning Process used to plan a commercial collection.

Retail therapy Shopping for leisure.

RTW Ready to wear.

Runway The showcase of designer collections. Also known as a catwalk.

Sampling Process of making initial prototype samples; forms part of range planning.

SBO Sales-based ordering: the use of EPOS data to generate an order for future stock requirements.

Smart fabric Fabric with a special finish, such as waterproof or technical fabrics for sportswear.

Social media Online interaction through websites such as Instagram, Twitter or Facebook.

Specification (spec) sheet Technical garment diagram supplied to manufacturers.

SNBN See Now Buy Now – selling technique direct from catwalk, developed by luxury brands.

SWOT Strengths, weaknesses, opportunities and threats: an internal business analysis model.

The Ten Ps The marketing mix.

USP Unique selling point: a feature of a company or product that differentiates it from similar companies or products.

Vintage Retro or antique fashion with value.

WTO World Trade Organization: an organization that intends to supervise and liberalize international trade.

Zeitgeist Capturing the spirit of the moment.

AGCAS editors, 'Job profile Retail merchandiser', AGCAS Graduate Prospects Ltd, 2019.
Available online:
https://www.prospects.ac.uk/job-profiles/retail-merchandiser (accessed 20 May 2020).

Bell, D., *The Coming of Post-Industrial Society*, Basic Books, 1987.

Bevan, J., *The Rise & Fall of Marks & Spencer. . . And How it Rose Again*, Profile Books, 2007.

Black, S., *Eco-Chic: The Fashion Paradox*, Black Dog Publishing, 2006.

BoF, and McKinsey & Company, 'The State of Fashion 2017', *The Business of Fashion*, McKinsey & Company, 2016.
Available online:
https://www.mckinsey.com/~/media/McKinsey/Industries/Retail/Our%20Insights/The%20state%20of%20fashion/The-state-of-fashion-2017-McK-BoF-report.ashx (accessed 20 May 2020).

Borden, N. H., *The Concept of the Marketing Mix*, 1965.

Brannon, E. L., *Fashion Forecasting: Research, Analysis, and Presentation*, Fairchild Books, 2005.

Burns, L., *The Fashion Business*, Fairchild Books, 2011.

Christopher, M., *Logistics and Supply Chain Management*, Financial Times/Prentice Hall, 2007.

Common Objective, CO, 'Apparel Production: Fibre to Fabric to Fashion', CO Data, 2018.
Available online:
https://www.commonobjective.co/article/apparel-production-fibre-to-fabric-to-fashion (accessed 20 May 2020).

Drucker, P., *The Effective Executive*, Harper Business, 2006.

Easey, M, *Fashion Marketing*, John Wiley and Sons, 2002.

Ethical Trading Initiative, 'The ETI Base Code', ETI, 2018.
Available online:
https://www.ethicaltrade.org/sites/default/files/shared_resources/ETI%20Base%20Code%20%28English%29.pdf (accessed 20 May 2020).

Gladwell, M., *The Tipping Point: How Little Things Can Make a Big Difference*, Abacus, 2008.

Goworek, H., *Fashion Buying*, John Wiley and Sons, 2007.

Hale, A., and Wills, J., *Threads of Labour*, Wiley-Blackwell, 2002.

Hamel, G. and Prahalad, C. K., *Competing for the Future*, Harvard Business School Press, 1994.

Holland, G. and Jones, R., *Trend Forecasting*, Bloomsbury Press, 2017.

Jackson, T. and Shaw, D., *Mastering Fashion Buying & Merchandising Management*, Palgrave Macmillan, 2005.

Johnson.G. and Scholes, P., *Exploring Corporate Strategy*, Prentice Hall, 2005.

Jong, Joanne Yulan, *The Fashion Switch*, Rethink Press, 2017.

Lee, A., 'Triple A Supply Chains: Supply chain agility, adaptability and alignment: empirical evidence from the Indian auto components industry,' *International Journal of Operations and Production Management*, (2008), 38 (1). pp. 129-148.

McGoldrick, P., *Retail Marketing*, McGraw-Hill Higher Education, 2002.

Petro, G., www.firstinsight.com

Porter, M., *Competitive Advantage*, Free Press, 1996.

Rieple, A., and Gander, J., 'Product development within a clustered environment: The case of apparel design firms,' *Creative Industries Journal 2* (December 2009), (3):273-289 .

Ries, A., and Trout, J., *Differentiate or Die: Survival in Our Era of Killer Competition*, John Wiley and Sons, 1992.

STYLUS.com, 'Dynamic Youth: Gen Z', STYLUS, 2019.
Available online:
https://www.stylus.com/dynamic-youth-gen-z (accessed 20 May 2020).

Sustainable Apparel Coalition, 'The Higg Index', The SAC website.
Available online:
https://apparelcoalition.org/the-higg-index/ (accessed 20 May 2020).

Thomas, D., *Deluxe: How Luxury Lost its Lustre*, Penguin, 2007.

Trott, P., *Innovation Management and New Product Development*, Financial Times/ Prentice Hall, 2007.

Tungate, M., *Fashion Brands: Branding Style from Armani to Zara*, Kogan Page, 2006.

Vejlgaard, H., *Anatomy of a Trend*, McGraw-Hill, 2007.

Yuri S., and Buchanan-Oliver, M., 'Luxury branding: the industry, trends, and future conceptualisations,' *Asia Pacific Journal of Marketing and Logistics* Vol. 27 No. 1,pp. 82-98, Emerald Group Publishing Limited, 2015.

www.acid.eu.com

www.burberry.com

www.businessoffashion.com

www.clothesource.net

www.coolhunting.com

www.datamonitor.com

www.edited.com

www.ethicaltrade.org

www.fakesareneverinfashion.com

www.firstinsight.com

www.guardian.co.uk

www.harrods.com

www.kering.com

www.labourbehindthelabel.org

www.louisvuitton.com

www.matchesfashion.com

www.mintel.com

www.nytimes.com

www.promostyl.com

www.prospects.ac.uk

www.ralphlauren.com

www.richinsight.com

www.steventai.co.uk

www.style.com

www.stylus.com

www.thebritishhouse.com.cn

www.trendhunter.com

www.vogue.com

www.wgsn.com

www.wto.org

www.wwd.com

www.ukft.org

Page numbers in italics refer to illustrations.

3D printed clothing, iv, 100, *101*, 102

Abellan, Sita, 58, *59*
Abloh, Virgil, 27, 131, 136
ACFDA, 143
ACID, 138
Acme, 78
Adidas, 27, 69, 102, 133
agent, 97
agility, 96
AIDA model, *133*, 152
Aiko, 78
Alaverdian, Natalia, 51
Alfred Dunhill, 145
Alger, Paul, 139–143
Alibaba, 86
Alice + Olivia, 78
All Saints, 10
Ally Cappellino, 139
Amazon, *15*, 84, 86, 130
Amed, Imran, *88*
Anthropologie, 10
Armani, 4, 144
artificial intelligence (AI), 102
Asda, 110
ASOS, 10, 84, 110, 115
Association of German Fashion and Textile Designers, 143
A.W.A.K.E., 51

Baby boomers, 126, 152
Balenciaga, 2, 4, 28
Balmain, 2, 4, 10, 36, 76, 130, *131*, 138
Bangladesh, 104, *109*, 114, 141
Bazaar (magazine), 134
Beagent, Tom, *117*
Beckham, Victoria, 12, 30
Benetton, 40
Beyonce, 133
Biba, 4
Bicester Village, 73
Bizzarri, Marco, *88*
Blockchain, 98

bloggers, vi, 5, 18, 21
Boden, 10, 70, *70*, 110
Bonobos, 74
born global, 74
Boston Consulting Group (BCG), 48
brands, 8, 123–49
    building, 127
    communications, 133
    customer profiling, 124–6
    extension and layering, 130–1
    fast fashion, 129–33
    luxury, 127–8, *129*
    mass market, 129–33
    protection, 136–8
    storytelling and promotion, 134, 136
    value, 131, 133
Branson, Cecile, 51
bridge lines, 130, 131, 152
British Fashion Council (BFC), 140, 143
British House, Beijing, 81, *122*, 123, *144*, 144–8, *145*, *146*, *148*
Browns, 81, 141
Brun, Alessandro, 7
Buchanan-Oliver, Margo, 128
Burberry, *6*, 38, 69, 72, 133, 141, 144
Burstein, Joan, 81
business model, See Now Buy Now (SNBN), 6
Business News Daily (magazine), 48
buyers, *17*
    fashion buying as career, 79
    renowned, 81
    responsibilities of, 79–80
    role of, 79–81
buying FOB (freight on board), 97, 152

C&A, 142
Calvin Klein, 4, 10
Cambridge satchel company, 146

career
    fashion buying, 79
    fashion merchandising, 82
case studies
    British House, Beijing, 144–8
    EDITED, 28–31
    Farfetch, 87–9
    Kering Group, 117–19
    MATCHESFASHION.COM, 53–62
cash cows, 48
Cashmere, 118
Cattrall, Kim, *13*
cause-related marketing (CRM), 102, 107, 152
celebrity culture, 136
celebrity designers, 27, 30
Celine, *129*
Central America, 104
CFDA (Council for Designers of America), 143, 152
Chalhoub Group, 87
Chanel, 2, 4, 6, 87, *128*, 138
Chapman, Ruth, 53, 61
Chapman, Tom, 53
Chelsea Girl, 4
Chen, Daniel, 140
China, 103, 109–10, 115, 144–7
Christian Dior, 2, *3*, 4, 10, 138
Christian Louboutin, 11, *11*, 73
Christopher, Martin, 95
Christopher Kane, 55, 76
Chromat Adrenaline Dress, 100, *101*
circular economy, concept of, viii
Claudie Pierlot, 78
Clothesource, 104, 114–16
Coca Cola, 22
Cocosa and BrandAlley, 73
colour forecasting, EDITED, 29
colour information, 16
Comite Colbert, 138
Common Objective (CO), 109
communications, brand, 133
comparative shopping, 16, 152
competition, 147

Competitive Advantage (Porter), *67*
Comptoir des Cotonniers, 78
computer-aided design (CAD), 38, 46, *47*
concessions, 72, 152
Conde Nast, 89
Converse, 38
cool hunting, 22–3, 152
copycat, 5, 6
corporate social responsibility (CSR), 107–8, 114, 120, 152
Corso Como, 81, *81*
Costume Institute Gala, Metropolitan Museum of Art, *23*
cotton harvest, Turkey, *111*
Cottonopolis, 95
Coulter, Cher, 62
Counterfeit Museum, 138
Courbet, Gustave, 136
couture, 2, 4
COVID-19 pandemic, 150
critical path, fashion, viii, ix, 41–2
CSR (corporate social responsibility), 107–8, 114, 120, 152
customer, behaviour and segmentation, 20
customer profiling, 124–6

Darris, Pauline, *105*
Daveu, Marie Claire, 110, 117, *117*
Derek Lam, 73
design brief, 152
designers
    fashion at work, *20*
    leaders, 10
    mavericks, 8
    outlets, 73
    reproducers, 10
    textile fair, *21*
    typology, 7–8
    workplace, x
digital marketing, 60
Dior, 4, 10, 138
directional shopping, 16
direct supply, 97, 152
Doddle, 85
dogs, 48

Dolce & Gabbana, 4
Donegar, 22
Dover Street Market, 81
Dream Assembly, 87, 88
Dream Museum, 89
Drexler, Millard 'Mickey', 78
drop model, 61, 152
drops of product, 40
Drucker, Peter, 10

Easey, Mike, 71
E-bay, 85
economies of scale, 71
Ede & Ravenscroft, 144
EDITED, 22, 28–31
electronic word of mouth (E-WOM), 123
Elkington, John, 112
ethical issues, 107
Ethical Trading Initiative (ETI), 110, 152

Fabscrap, *108*
Facebook, 136, 140
Farfetch, 72, 78, 81, 87–9, *88*, 130, 141
fashion, v, 1, 151
fashion business, 32
    as critical path, viii
    designers, v
    role of design in, 36–9
fashion buyer, 79
Fashion Concierge, 87
fashion critical path, viii, ix, 41–2
fashion design studio, *49*
fashion industry, v
fashion merchandising, 82
The Fashion Switch (Jong), v
fashion technologist, *49*
Fast, Mark, 81
fast fashion, vii, 4–6, 39, *48*, 95–9, 120
    4Rs, 95
    brands, 129–33
    designers, 10
    term, 96
Fast Retailing, 69
Federation de la Haute Couture et de la Mode, 143
Fendi, 38
Fenty, 136

Field, Pat, 12, *13*
Fila, 38
Fillis, Hannah, 53, 55, 60, 62
First Insight, 102
Five Forces model, *67*
Flanagan, Mike, 114
footfall, 72
Ford, Tom, 10
forecasting, 12
Forever 21, *5*, 10, 70, 74
for-profit industry, 1
Fowler, Julia, 28
FoxTown, 73
franchises, 72
Fred Perry, 139
Frings, Gini Stephens, 4
Frownie, Ally, 39
Fujiwara, Hiroshi, 40
full-service vendor (FSV), 97, 152

Galliano, John, 8, 50, 81
Gap, 4, 69, 78, 110
garment factory, *106*
garment specifications, 46, 47–9
Geldof, Pixie, *125*
generational cohort, 124, 126, 152
Gen X, 126, 152
Gen Y, 126, 152
Gen Z, 28, 117–19, 126, 152
Gerber, Kaia, 12
Giambatissta Valli, H&M collaboration with, *34*, 35, *45*, 129
Gilt Groupe, 73
Giorgio Armani, 4, 144
Givenchy, 2, 4
Globalization, fashion supply chains, 105, 107
glossary, 152–3
Goddard, Molly, 53
Gordon-Smith, Emily, 25–7
Gosha Rubchinskiy, 38
Goyard, 141
Grey Fox, 143
Griffin Laundry, 139
Gryphon, 78
Gucci, 2, 4, *5*, 8, 12, 28, 55, 70, 72, 74, 118, 131
Gucci Advent New York, *119*
guerilla stores, 73

H&M, 5, 10, 36, 51, 69, 74, 76, 79, 107, 131, 142
  collaboration with Giambatissta Valli, *34*, 35, *45*, 129
  pop-up store, *45*
Hadid, Gigi, 12
Halpern, Michael, 62
Hanes Brands, 69
Harrods brands, 144–6
Harvey Nichols, 87
haute couture, 2, 152
Heatherwick, Thomas, *78*
Hermès, 69, 70, 129, 138
Hickey Freeman, 144
Higg Index, 112
Highgrove products, 145–6
high-street revolution, 4–6
Holland, G., 23, 24
House of Fraser, 84
Hudson Yards New York, *78*
Hugo Boss, 73, 145
Hurtley, Richard, 84–6
Hussein Chalayan, 139
Hyères Fashion Festival, 50

idea generation, research and, 11–12
Ilincic, Roksanda, *64*, 65
India, 103
Inditex, 69, 110
Industrial Revolution, 95
influencers, 5, 18
innovations, 85
Instagram, 136, 140
Intel's Curie Module, 100, *101*
international brands, 130
International Labour Organization (ILO), 108
interpreters, 10
Intertek, 47
interviews
  Alger, Paul, 139–43
  Gordon-Smith, Emily, 25–7
  Hurtley, Richard, 84–6
  Leffman, Liz, 114–16
  Tai, Steven, 50–2
Issa, Caroline, *70*
Italy, 104

Jay-Z, 12, 27
J.Crew, 78
JD.com, 87

Jeff Griffin, 139
Jenner, Kendall, *34*, 35
Jenny Packham, 139
Jerome, Ulrich, 53
Jigsaw, 80, *80*
Jil Sander, 73
Jimmy Choo, 131
Joe Public, 139
Johansson, Ann Sofie, 36, *37*
John Lewis, 70, 84, 115
John Smedley, *94*, 104, 146
Jonathan Saunders, 144
Jones, R, 23, 24
Jong, Joanne Yulan, v, 134
Joshua Ellis Cashmere, 146
just in time (JIT), 98
JW Anderson, 38

Kane, Christopher, 81
Kardashians, 30
Kardashian West, Kim, 28, *31*
Karen Millen, 10
Karl Lagerfeld, 36, 76
Kate Spade, 134
Katharine Hamnett, 60
Kering Group, 69, 107, 110–11, 117–19
  future challenges, 118–19
  logo, *118*
key opinion leaders (KOLs), vi, 21, 60, 134
key performance indicators (KPIs), 112
Kiki de Montparnasse, 78
Kingham, Natalie, 53, 81
Kobori, Michael, vi, vii, 107
Koenig, Aylin, 56, *57*
The Kooples, 78
Kurkova, Karolina, *23*

Labour Behind the Label, 109
Lacroix, 50
Lane Crawford, 142, 147
Lau, Susanna, 18, *19*
Lauterborn (4Cs) model, 42, *44*
LBrands, 69
leaders, 10
leanness, 96
Le Coq Sportif, *103*
Leffman, Liz, 114–16
Levi Strauss, 4, 22, 25, *73*, 110
Li and Fung, 97
licensing, 72

lifestyle change, 126
local manufacturing, *103*
logistics, 85, 113
Louis Vuitton, 27, 38, 40, 70, 74, 128, 131, 136, *137*, 138
Luxottica, 69
luxury brands, 127–8, *129*
LVMH, 69, 136

M&S, 25, 115
Macarthur, Ellen, viii
McCabe, Yimei, 144–5
'Made for Outlet', 73
magazine culture, 148
Makaroff, Miranda, 58, *59*
Mannino, Kim, *24*
Margaret Howell, 139
Margiela, 36
market analysis and research, 12
marketing, 148
marketing mix
  people, 76, 78–83
  place, 72–4
  position, 71
  price, 74–6
marketplace, 18, 85
Marks and Spencers, *106*
Martin, Marci, 48
Mary Katrantzou, 139
Mary Quant, 4
Massenet, Natalie, 89
mass market, brands, 129–33
masstige, 4, 105
Matches, 10, 81, 141
MATCHESFASHION.COM, 53–62, *64*
  brand selection process, 56, 60
  content creation, 61
  digital and physical marketing, 60
  global brands, 55–6
  global collections, 62
  global luxury success story, 55
  international events, 62
  new designers, 55
  personalization and service, 61–2
  point of difference, 62
  RAEY private label, 61

MATCHESFASHION.COM
   (continued)
     Townhouse store, 53, 56
     vision statement, 55
mavericks, 8
Max Mara, 73
megatrends, 18, 152
merchandiser
     fashion merchandising as
       career, 82
     responsibilities of, 82–3
     role of, 82–3
Mexico, 104
Michael Kors, 69
Michele, Alessandro, 8, 10, 12,
     28, 131
micro trend, 152
Minkoff, Rebecca, 6
Miro, Alba, 134, *135*
mock-up, 46
Moghaddam, Kaveh, *5*
Molly Goddard, *54*, 55
Moncler, 40, *58*
Montinar, Sabina, *108*
moodboards, *9*, 38, 152
Morency, Christopher, 53
Morgan, Andrew, vi
Moschino, 36, *37*, 131
Mulberry, 141
Mullins, Alex, 51
Multi-Fibre Arrangement
     (MFA), 95, 152

Neiman Marcus, 74
Net a Porter, 10
Neves, José, 78, 87, *88*, 89
New Look, *3*, 110
Next, 69, 110, 115
NGOs (non-governmental
     organizations), 108–10,
     152
Nigel Cabourn, 139
Nike, 22, 69, 74, 133
Nous Paris, 81

obsolescence, 71
One Ocean One Planet, *125*
online discount outlets/clubs,
     73
online retail, 73
opening price point (OPP), 75,
     152
open to buy (OTB), 82, 153

Optimized Line Planning (OLP),
     102
outsourcing, 111, 113, 114–15

Palace, 38
Pandora, 69
Parker, Suzy, *3*
Partnership for Cleaner Textiles
     (PaCT), 107
Paul Smith, 139
pay-per-click adverts (PPC), 60
Peclers, 22
PESTEL model, 18, *67*, 68, *68*,
     153
Petro, Greg, 102
Pinault, Francois-Henri, 117,
     117
Planned Obsolescence, 39
planning, 40, 46, 51, 63
Polo Ralph Lauren, 38
pop-up shop, 73, 153
Porter, Michael, *67*, 70
Powell, Jamie, 144–5
Prada, 55, 56, *57*
prêt-à-porter (ready-to-wear),
     2, 4, 153
Prene, 76
pricing, 74–6, *75*, 119
Primark, *45*, 70, 74, 110, 115
private label, 36
product development, 35, 63,
     153
     initial concepts, 38–9
     private label, 36, 38
     range plan, 39
production line, *103*
product mix, 40–6, 63
     basics or core items, 44, *45*
     drops of product in season,
       40
     fashion items, 44, 46
     fashion product critical
       path, 41–2
     Lauterborn (4Cs) model,
       42, *44*
     range plan, 40
     ten Ps, 42, *43*
Proenza Schouler, 76, *77*, 78
Promostyl, 21
promotion, brand, 134, 136
Proud, Rachel, 61
Pugh, Gareth, 81
Puma, 27

question marks, 48–9
quick response (QR), 96, 153

radio frequency identification
     (RFID), 89, *99*
Raey private label, *38*, 61
Raf Simons, 10
Rag & Bone, 78, *132*
Ralph Lauren, 4, *42*, 73, 130
Rampant Sporting, 84
Rana Plaza disaster, 114
range plan, 40, 46, 51–2, 63,
     79, 153
ready-to-wear, 2, 4, 153
The Real Real, 74
recycled fabrics, *108*
Reiss, 10, 110
Rent the Runway, 74
reproducers, 10
research
     idea generation and, 11–12
     market analysis and, 12
retailer, for-profit industry, 1
retail experts, 78
retail internationalization, 74
retail positioning, 71
retail selling price (RSP), 75
retail strategy, 66, 90
     Five Forces model, *67*
     future of, 86
     implementing, 69
     Porter's, 70
retail therapy, 65
RFID (radio frequency
     identification), 89, *99*
Richard Quinn, *58*
Richemont, 69
Rich Insight, 84–6
Rihanna, 12, *14*, 136
risk management, supply
     chain, 111–12
Rodarte, 62, 73
Rolex, 128
Rosen, Andrew, 78
Rousteing, Oliver, 10, 130, *131*
Rovira, Ines, 134, *135*
runway, 6, 28, *34*, 35, *54*, 55,
     76, *77*, 127, *131*, *132*,
     153

Sandro, 78
scarcity effect, 102
Scott, Jeremy, 36, *37*

season neutral strategy, 27
See Now Buy Now (SNBN), 6, 7, 16, 39, 102, 123, 153
semiotics, 133
Seo, Yuri, 128
Sheldon, Fran, 22, 28–9
Sherman, Lauren, 6
shopping, 65
shop within a shop, 72
smart fabrics, 49, 153
Smith, Tilly Macallister, *38*
Snapchat, 136
social media, 18, 26, 60, 119, 134, 136, 140, 153
specialist fabrics, 49
specification (spec) sheet, 39, 46–9, 63, 153
Sri Lanka, *92*, 93, 103–4, *106*
stars, 48
Stella McCartney, 50, 115, 139
steventai, 50–2
Store of the Future, 87, 88–9
Store X Berlin, 81
Storey, Robert, 56
storytelling, 134, 136
street style in Berlin, 134, *135*
Stylus, 22, 25–7
Stylus.com, 119
Superdry, 72
Supply Chain 4.0, 98
supply chain management (SCM), 93, 95, 120
supply chains, 94–5
    fashion SCM strategy, 96–7
    globalization effects, 105, 107
    global sourcing and world class, 100–7
    goal of digital, 99
    lean and agile, 96
    logistics and outsourcing in, 113
    relationships in SCM, 97
    risk measures and controls in, 111–12
    4Rs, 95
    supplier types, 97
    sustainability in fashion, 107–11, 117
    technology in, 98
    trends and drivers of change, 98
    verticality in, 98

Supreme, 38
Susie Bubble, 18, *19*
sustainability, vi, vii
    fashion supply chains, 107–11
    Kering Group, 117–19
Sustainable Apparel Coalition (SCA), 112
SWOT diagram micro business factors, *67*, 153
Symonds, 139

Tai, Steven, 50–2, 140
Target, 25, 70
Ted Baker, 10, 72, 139
Tesco, 110
textile fair, *21*
textile industry, 94–5
    factory workers, *94*
    workers in Bangladesh, *109*
Thefashionlaw.com, 137
Tiffany, 128
Tim Everest, 141
tipping point, 22
Tisci, Riccardo, 133
TJMaxx X, 69
toile, 46
Ton, Tommy, 53
top design houses, 25
Topshop, 5, 10, 76
trade fairs/show, 16, *17*, *24*
trend forecasting, 21–4, 26–7
    EDITED case study, 28–31
Trend Union, 22
Triple-A Supply Chain, 100
triple bottom line, 112
The True Cost (film), vi
Tsao, Andrea, 53
Turkey, 104, *111*
Twitter, 136, 140
typology, designer, 7–8

UK (United Kingdom), 104
UK Fashion and Textile Association, 104
UK fashion and textiles organization (UKFT), 139–43
Undercover, 51
Uniqlo, 69, *69*, 74, 107, 129
USA, 104–5
USP (unique selling point), 97, 150, 153

Vanity Fair (magazine), 38
Vanity Fair Corp, 69
Veja Shoes, *105*
Vente-Privee, 73
Ventrillon, Mati, 6
Versace, 131
Verticality, supply chains, 98
Vestiare, 74
Vetements, 38
Viktor & Rolf, 50
vintage retail, 74
visual merchandising, *66*
Vivienne Westwood, 8, 38, 139, 142
Vogue (magazine), 38, 134
VOICES, *88*

Walpole Group, 138
Wang, Haizhen, 140
Warhol, Andy, 11
Wa-tat, Yan, *99*
Waterhouse, Suki, 62
Watts, Geoff, 28
Wechat, 52, 140, 147, 148
West, Kanye, 12, *14*, 30, *31*, 136
WGSN, 21, *24*
Whatsapp, 52
Whayeb, Besma, *125*
when it's gone it's gone (WIGIG), 102
World Bank, 108
World Trade Organization (WTO), 110, 153
Worth, Charles Frederick, v, 2

Yamamoto, Yohji, 50
Yeezy, *14*, 30
Yves Saint Laurent (YSL), 2, 4, 55, 118, 128, 138

Zalando, 73, 85, 130, 134, *135*
Zalora, 73
Zara, 5, 10, 25, 40, *48*, 69, 74, 96, 107, 110, 129, 131, 142
zeitgeist, 12, 30, 153
Zhang, Huishan, 140
Zhi, Xu, 140

1.1 Photo by Paco Freire/SOPA Images/Light Rocket via Getty Images
1.2 Photo by Horst P. Horst/Conde Nast via Getty Images
1.3 Photo by Christian Vierig/Getty Images
1.4 Photo by Victor VIRGILE/Gamma-Rapho via Getty Images
1.5 DIAGRAM DESIGNER TYPOLOGY
1.6 Photo by Lightfield Studios for Getty Images
1.7 Photo by Angela Weiss AFP via Getty Images
1.8 Photo by MPI67/Bauer-Griffin/GC Images via Getty Images
1.9 Photo by Jim Spellman/WireImage
1.10 Photo by Onnie A Koski/Getty Images
1.11 Photo credit JACQUES DEMARTHON/AFP via Getty Images
1.12 Photo credit JACQUES DEMARTHON/AFP via Getty Images
1.13 Photo by Claudio Lavenia/Getty Images
1.14 Photo by suedhang via Getty Images
1.15 Photo by Taylor Hill/FilmMagic via Getty Images
1.16 Photo credit JACQUES DEMARTHON/AFP via Getty Images
1.17 Photo by Daniel Pier/NurPhoto via Getty Images
1.18 Photo by Cansin Soyer/Getty Images for IMG
1.19 Photo by Daniel Zuchnik/Getty Images

2.1 Photo by Daniele Venturelli/WireImage
2.2 Photo by Jamie McCarthy/Getty Images
2.3 Photo by Kirstin Sinclair/Getty Images
2.4 Photo by Dave M. Benett/Getty Images
2.5 DIAGRAM LAUTERBORN MODEL
2.6 DIAGRAM 10P's
2.7 Photo by Stefania M. D'Alessandro/Getty Images for H&M
2.8 Photo by Ulrich Baumgarten via Getty Images
2.9 Photo by trumzz for Getty Images
2.10 Photo by John Keeble/Getty Images
2.11 Photo by Monty Rakusen for Getty Images
2.12 Photo by John Phillips/BFC/Getty Images for BFC
2.13 Photo by Jeremy Moeller/Getty Images
2.14 Photo by Darren Gerrish/Getty Images
2.15 Photo by Noam Galai/Getty Images for The Cultivist
2.16 Photo by Darren Gerrish/Getty Images

3.1 Photo by David M. Benett/Dave Benett/Getty Images
3.2 Photo by Solstock via Getty Images
3.3 DIAGRAM FIVE FORCES
3.4 DIAGRAM SWOT
3.5 DIAGRAM PESTEL
3.6 Photo by Zhang Peng/LightRocket via Getty Images
3.7 Photo by Kirstin Sinclair/Getty Images
3.8 Photo by Alex Tai/SOPA Images/LightRocket via Getty Images
3.9 DIAGRAM PRICE MATRIX
3.10 Photo by Victor VIRGILE/Gamma-Rapho via Getty Images
3.11 Photo by Alexi Rosenfeld/Getty Images
3.12 Photo by Ian Gavan/BFC/Getty Images
3.13 Photo by Thomas Vilhelm/Cover/Getty Images
3.14 Photo by John Phillips/Getty Images for The Business of Fashion

4.1 Photo credit Ishara S. KODIKARA/AFP via Getty Images
4.2 Photo by George Freston/Getty Images
4.3 Photo credit ANTHONY WALLACE/AFP via Getty Images
4.4 Photo by Ethan Miller/Getty Images
4.5 Photo credit FRANCOIS NASCIMBENI/AFP via Getty Images
4.6 Photo by Edward Berthelot/Getty Images
4.7 Ishara S. KODIKARA/AFP via Getty Images
4.8 Photo credit Ishara S. KODIKARA/AFP via Getty Images
4.9 Photo credit DON EMMERT/AFP via Getty Images
4.10 Photo by Mehedi Hasan/NurPhoto via Getty Images
4.11 Photo by Ibrahim Erikan/Anadolu Agency via Getty Images
4.12 Photo credit FRANCOIS GUILLOT/AFP via Getty Images
4.13 Photo Igor Golovniov/SOPA Images/LightRocket via Getty Images
4.14 Photo credit DON EMMERT/AFP via Getty Images

5.1 Photo credit The British House
5.2 Photo by Lisa Wiltse/Corbis via Getty Images

5.3 Photo credit STEPHANE DE SAKUTIN/AFP via Getty Images

5.4 Photo by MIGUEL MEDINA/AFP via Getty Images

5.5 Photo by Victor VIRGILE/Gamma-Rapho via Getty Images

5.6 Photo by Peter White/FilmMagic

5.7 DIAGRAM AIDA

5.8 Photo by Christian Vierig/Getty Images for Zalando

5.9 Photo credit GABRIEL BOUYS/AFP via Getty Images

5.10 Photo credit FRANCOIS GUILLOT/AFP via Getty Images

5.11 Photo credit The British House

5.12 Photo credit The British House

5.13 Photo credit The British House

5.14 Photo credit The British House

This second edition is dedicated to all my students across the world from whom I have learned so much. I would also like to thank those that have contributed their valuable time to this book through their generous time spent being interviewed.

They are: Emily Gordon Smith, Fran Sheldon, Steven Tai, Hannah Fillis, Paul Alger MBE, Richard Hurtley, Liz Leffman, Jamie Powell and everyone at Bloomsbury, especially Georgia Kennedy, Faith Marsland and Belinda Campbell.

Also, my colleagues at the University of Westminster for their supportive advice, especially Caroline Curtis and Nicola Mansfield. A final thank you goes to a dear friend and writer Elaine Swift for her help and guidance through the process of this second edition.